"Dr. Naughton brings to life the fundamental insights of the Catholic social tradition in its relation to business. Drawing upon the Catholic understanding of vocation, human dignity, common good, subsidiarity, solidarity, justice, and universal destination of the goods of the earth, he relates these principles to the commonplace practices of business—discerning your call, designing good jobs to exercise gifts and talents of workers, creating goods that truly are 'good,' paying just wages, and other important business practices."

— CARDINAL PETER K.A. TURKSON —
President, Dicastery for Promoting Integral
Human Development

"This little book conveys practical wisdom about the all-too-scattered works and days of our lives. It is a veritable retreat for serious businesspeople."

— RUSSELL HITTINGER —
William K. Warren Professor of Catholic Studies,
University of Tulsa

"This is a wise book that reorients work to the service of what matters: a life of joy shared with other people and with God. Michael Naughton makes this lofty ideal eminently practical, and never recommends anything that he has not practiced himself. Best of all, the book is not a guilt trip but a portal to happiness. To anyone who has ever felt overworked, overly busy, or distracted by the demands of social media, this book will seem like water in the desert."

— WILLIAM T. CAVANAUGH —
Professor, DePaul University

"In an emerging literature on the theme of meaningful work, Naughton's *Getting Work Right* will have a preeminent place. His insight that meaningful work is bound at its roots with meaningful leisure—that the work week and the day of rest give meaning to each other—offers readers an intelligent, personal, and practical guide to living."

— KENNETH GOODPASTER —
Professor Emeritus, University of St. Thomas, Minnesota

·❧·

LIVING FAITH

**SERIES EDITOR: FR. DAVID VINCENT MECONI, S.J.**
Fr. David Vincent Meconi, S.J., is a Jesuit priest and professor of theology at Saint Louis University where he also serves as the Director of the Catholic Studies Centre. He is the editor of *Homiletic and Pastoral Review* and has published widely in the areas of Church history and Catholic culture. He holds the pontifical license in Patristics from the University of Innsbruck in Austria, and the D.Phil. in Ecclesiastical History from the University of Oxford.

## ABOUT THE SERIES

The great Christian Tradition has always affirmed that the world in which we live is a reflection of its divine source, a place perhaps torn apart by sin but still charged with busy and bustling creatures disclosing the beautiful presence of God. The *Living Faith* series consists of eminent Catholic authors who seek to help Christians navigate their way in this world. How do we understand objective truth in a culture insistent on relativism? How does one evangelize in a world offended when invited to something higher? How do we understand sin and salvation when so many have no real interest in becoming saints? The *Living Faith* series will answer these and numerous other questions Christians have today as they set out not only to live holy lives themselves, but to bring others to the fullness of life in Christ Jesus.

Published or Forthcoming

*The Adventure of Discipleship*
Daniel A. Keating

*Catholicism and Intelligence*
Fr. James V. Schall, S.J.

*The Family of God and How Christ Lives in His Church Today*
Carl E. Olson

*Jesus Christ in Islam and Christianity*
Fr. Mitch Pacwa, S.J.

*Apologetics and the Christian Imagination*
Holly Ordway

*Holiness and Living the Sacramental Life*
Fr. Philip-Michael Tangorra

*The Joyful Mystery: Field Notes Toward a Green Thomism*
Christopher J. Thompson

*Sanctity and Scripture*
Scott Hahn

*Catholic and at College*
Anne Carson Daly

*Living Grace & Deadly Sin: A Guide to Getting Our Souls Straight*
Fr. David Vincent Meconi, S.J.

# GETTING WORK RIGHT

# GETTING WORK RIGHT

## Labor and Leisure in a Fragmented World

### MICHAEL J. NAUGHTON

EMMAUS ROAD
PUBLISHING

Steubenville, Ohio
www.emmausroad.org

Emmaus Road Publishing
1468 Parkview Circle
Steubenville, Ohio 43952

Library of Congress Control Number: 2019907615
ISBN: 978-1-949013-55-9

Cover image: *Summer: The Harvesters* (1623) by Pieter Breughel the Younger

Cover design and layout by Emily Feldkamp

To Teresa, my wife, whose wisdom and counsel has guided me for over thirty years.

# TABLE OF CONTENTS

Foreword                                                    i

Introduction                                                vii

**I. The Challenge of Integrity**                           1

CHAPTER ONE
The Divided Life: A Tale of Two Adams                        3

CHAPTER TWO
Small Work and Shallow Leisure                              19

CHAPTER THREE
The Logic of Gift:
The Call to Give and Receive                                35

**II. Labor**                                               51

CHAPTER FOUR
The Purpose of Business:
Defining the Good Business Does                             53

CHAPTER FIVE
Good Work:
Gift Recognition and Coordination                          77

CHAPTER SIX
Good Goods: Goods That Are Truly Good                       99

CHAPTER SEVEN
Good Wealth: Its Creation and Distribution                 121

**III. Leisure**                                          143

CHAPTER EIGHT
The Power of Sunday: Holy Rest                             145

**Epilogue**                                              169

·⟡·

FOREWORD

# CARDINAL PETER K.A. TURKSON

PRESIDENT,
DICASTERY FOR PROMOTING INTEGRAL
HUMAN DEVELOPMENT
HOLY SEE

In 2011, my office, which at the time was called the Pontifical Council for Justice and Peace, convened a seminar of a group of scholars and practitioners to discuss the implications of Pope Benedict's encyclical letter, *Caritas in veritate*, for business. One of those persons at the seminar was the author of this book, Dr. Michael Naughton. The seminar produced a rich discussion of theological and practical insights on the vocation of the business leader. From this seminar, we organized a committee under the very competent leadership of Dr. Naughton to produce *Vocation of the Business Leader* in 2012.[1] I am grateful to

---

[1] Dicastery for Promoting Integral Human Development, *Vocation of the Business Leader*, https://www.stthomas.edu/media/catholic-studies/center/ryan/publications/publicationpdfs/vocationofthebusinessleaderpdf/FinalTextTheVocationoftheBusinessLeader.pdf

i

him and his committee.

This document distills the profound and extensive tradition of the social teachings of the Church as it relates to business. Since that time (its publication in 2012), *Vocation of the Business Leader* has been translated in over fifteen languages and it is currently in its 5th edition. It is used by business executives, faith groups, and universities to see and explore the implications of faith in the business world. *Vocation of the Business Leader* has also generated interest by other professionals to address the vocation of agricultural,[2] engineering, financial, and political leaders. It has been a fruitful document.

This book, *Getting Work Right: Labor and Leisure in a Fragmented World,* serves as an important and practical tool to help the faithful more deeply and personally consider the principles within *Vocation of the Business Leader.* Dr. Naughton brings to life the fundamental insights of the Catholic social tradition in its relation to business. Drawing upon the Catholic understanding of vocation, human dignity, common good, subsidiarity, solidarity, justice, and universal destination of the goods of the earth, he relates these principles to the commonplace practices of business—discerning your call, designing good jobs to exercise gifts and talents of workers, creating goods that

---

[2]   Cf. *Vocation of Agricultural Leader,* Catholic Rural Life, 2016. http://www.faithfoodenvironment.org/wp-content/uploads/2016/12/The-Vocation-of-the-Agricultural-Leader.pdf

truly are "good," paying just wages and other important business practices.

Jesus teaches us that faith is never a private reality restricted to small areas of our lives.[3] Faith is the yeast that is leaven for the whole of life, including business. Pope Francis well recognizes that business is a noble vocation, but he is concerned by the false ideal of personal or corporate gain to the detriment of all else. He calls business people to institutionalize the good in their organizations. Dr. Naughton gives us illustrative examples and cases of what this good can look like for businesses. He also realistically explains the tensions and challenges in bringing the good to bear in today's businesses.

Perhaps what is most refreshing about Dr. Naughton's book is the personal and practical tone of what he writes. This is not merely an academic exercise for him. As both the director of the Center for Catholic Studies at the University of St. Thomas as well as the board chair of Reell Precision Manufacturing, he brings together the theolog-

---

[3]  Cf. John Paul II, Homily at Beatification Mass of Adolph Kolping (October 27, 1991): "For him Christianity/the Christian faith should not be understood simply as a 'prayer room,' but inserted in the daily life and aimed at forming social reality. The places in which to exercise human and Christian responsibility are, for him, the family, the Church, work and politics" (Per lui il cristianesimo non doveva intendersi semplicemente come una 'stanza di preghiera,' ma inserito nel quotidiano e volto alla formazione della realtà sociale. I luoghi, in cui si deve esercitare la responsabilità umana e cristiana sono per lui: la famiglia, la Chiesa, il lavoro e la politica). My translation.

ical richness of our faith and the practical experience of what the good can look like daily in the world of business. This integration of faith and business is so desperately needed in a world that too often compartmentalizes life into discrete and separate units.

Most importantly, Dr. Naughton captures something that we are in danger of losing in the modern world. If we are to "get work right," we need to get leisure right. If we are to get Monday right, we have to get Sunday right. Our deepest identity as human beings is not found in our work, gender, ethnicity or race. Our deepest identity is found in the reality of the gift of life. We are created in God's image, where the Book of Genesis tells us we are not only made to work but also to rest. We are born not into a business but into a family—with family who, for many us, had us baptized. Here St. Augustine teaches us a great lesson. When he searches for his deepest identity, his inner domain, he finds not himself, but God. It is in God that Augustine comes to that universal claim: "Our heart is restless until it rests in you."

Our work is not our own. We need to go beyond our work as a job and career and see that each day we are called to bring the good news of the Gospel to work. This will not be done well unless we first receive the Gospel in prayer, in worship, in Word and Sacrament. All of us, whether cleric or lay, need to be people who *live faith* at work and bring our *living faith* to work, thereby making them more humane places.

God has given all of us a work to do, which he has not given to another, as John Henry Newman once put it. Yet often out of good will, we tend to focus only on what work we are to do, and unintentionally lose sight of the deeper transformation of life and purpose. The pattern of labor and leisure, of giving and receiving, of the active and contemplative life, is a key theme of this book that can help a reader not lose sight of this important truth. Rightly ordered labor and leisure give us roots in a world that too often only gives us cut flowers. I hope you find those deep roots for your life and that this book can be an aid to your search.

INTRODUCTION

This is a book about roots, about discovering the origins and foundations in how we are to work and rest. In particular, it is about being grounded in a faith that can answer our deeper questions of our practical life, an answer that centers on the integration of the active and contemplative life.

Our challenge, however, is that we live in a world of cut flowers—plants with no roots: a world of slogans, branding, and marketing. This world feeds us the idea that doing good is simply the achievement of our own individual will, accomplished without deeper changes to the habits of who we are as persons within institutions. And if we cannot get an individual to act well, we can socially reengineer ethics through rules and incentives.

An ethic, however, founded only on self-interest, utility, contracts, or even duty is prone to grow cold. Life grinds away too hard for such constructs to hold over a lifetime. Such ethical systems are too small for the human spirit; they do not have the roots to nourish our humanity whether in the family or in the workplace.

This world of cut flowers creates, in the words of C. S. Lewis, "men without chests," but we still expect virtue from them.[1] We unknowingly remove the ethical organ of humanity, yet naively demand its function. Particularly in the West, we too often believe that we can escape the deepest convictions of humanity, which are fundamentally spiritual and religious, but still remain ethical.

Perhaps this is so in part because the roots that faith and religion offer can make us uncomfortable. Will not reliance on a religious explanation be seen as too exclusive and dogmatic? After all, it will be claimed that faith, let alone Christian faith, does not have a monopoly on good work and good businesses. And surely Christians should not proselytize and impose their beliefs on others. While there is merit to these objections, I find that in practice the difficulty comes from the opposite direction.

The call of every Christian is to evangelize (not proselytize), to bring the Gospel to all of humanity, including the world of work and business. It means bringing criteria of judgment and principles of reflection whose roots run deep within the groundwork of reality—deeper than merely a market or a legal logic focused on choice, achievement, and compliance. The deeper logic the Christian brings is one of *gift*, a logic nurtured by the profound sense that we operate in a created order, which we can only receive in wonder and awe. It is only with this disposition that we can get to the roots of the matter, to the

---

[1]   C. S. Lewis, *The Abolition of Man* (New York: HarperOne, 2001), 26.

truest parts of what it means to be alive.

Yet, our contemporary culture frightens leaders away from expressing any kind of faith lest they be perceived as too "religious," "dogmatic," or "exclusive." There are few labels more dreaded than these in a pluralistic world. The fear of such labels paralyzes people of faith in their businesses and organizations, who then tend to accommodate to whatever values, strategies, or recent consultant fads the organization has set in motion. Rather than being a light to those around them, such leaders settle into the lowest common denominator of organizational groupthink. But surely we can do better than this.

T. S. Eliot wrote, "It may prove in the long run that the problems we have postponed or ignored, rather than those we have failed to attack successfully, will be the ones to return to plague us."[2] There is within the corporate world an increasing political correctness that has a deep hostility to anything religious. We have thus ignored the Gospel, thinking that we can be ethical on our own, that we can solve all our problems, that we can work out our own salvations. But we can't.

The fundamental thesis of this book is that we will not get our work right unless we get our leisure right. Leisure or rest here does not merely mean amusement or "time

---

[2] T. S. Elliot, *Christianity and Culture: The Idea of a Christian Society and Notes towards the Definition of Culture* (San Diego: Harcourt Brace Jovanovich, 1949), 5.

off"; but as Josef Pieper explained it, leisure is rather to be found in the soul that receives the reality of the world. Leisure can be expressed in many ways: in contemplation, in prayer, in silence, in the beauty of nature, in play, in art and music—wherever people foster the capacity to receive the world. But at the heart of leisure is worship—a claim that this world and all that is in it is good. It is good not because any person says so but because it has been created so.

This important relationship between work and leisure is not easily integrated, however. We face the particular temptation of the divided life (addressed in chapter one), which the Second Vatican Council called one of the "serious errors of our age." This problem of the divided life leads either to undervaluing our work by seeing it simply as a "job," or overvaluing our work by seeing it as a "career" that defines our identity (chapter two). A faith response means going beyond "job" and "career" and learning to see our work as a "calling" (chapter three). But this takes some exploring into human activity outside of work—in leisure: play, family time, Sunday worship, silence, prayer.

Chapter four focuses on what a good business looks like when vocation is taken seriously, answering questions about the specific "goods" that business accomplishes. The social teaching of the Church speaks of three such "goods": good work, good goods, and good wealth. Chapters five to seven examine each of these "goods" and give examples of how businesses and organizations can achieve them through innovative practices and policies.

The final chapter of the book extends the main thesis to the following proposition: if we do not get Sunday right, we will not get Monday—or any day of the workweek—right. Sunday, the Lord's Day, the Sabbath, expresses leisure in both rest and worship. It reveals the fundamental insight that we are made not only to work but also to rest and to worship. Drawing upon Augustine, Bishop Robert Barron has noted, "False worship leads to false social arrangements."[3] This is why we cannot be good leaders if we do not know how to worship. This may be the most controversial claim of the whole book.

This book has been in the making for the last ten years. Just as it takes a village to raise a child, it takes a community to write a book. In my case, this group of people has been a community of practitioners and scholars. As for practitioners, they include many: Kyle Smith, Bob Wahlstedt, Shari Erdman, Ed Mosel, Jack Field, and others from Reell Precision Manufacturing, where I have served on the board of directors for over ten years. I have also learned a tremendous amount of practical insight from UNIAPAC, a global faith and business group. I am partic-

---

[3]  Reverend Robert E. Barron, "Augustine's Critique of Rome: A Theological Reflection on Violence and Non-Violence" (address, John Carroll University, March 16, 2005), Prism (Summer 2005), 6, 8.

ularly indebted to Pierre Lecocq, Rolando Medeiros, and Jose Ignacio Mariscal. Many executives who have been involved in Catholic health care have been helpful in connecting the mission and practice, such as Bill Brinkman, Sr. Maureen McGuire, Celeste Mueller, Dean Maines, and others. I have been blessed by the incredible staff at Catholic Studies at the University of St. Thomas (MN) who incarnates the practical virtue of servant leadership on a daily basis. In particular, I am grateful to Mary Kay O'Rourke, Maureen Huss, Nancy Sannerud, Ann Serdar, and Jessica Zittlow Aleman. As for scholars, they include the founder of Catholic Studies, Don Briel (†), as well as Robert Kennedy, John Boyle, Ken Goodpaster, Msgr. Martin Schlag, Fr. Michael Keating, Jeanne Buckeye, John McVea, Brian Shapiro, and many others. Finally, a special thanks to Katie Takats and Mary Catherine Adams for their editorial assistance and to my student workers, Rebekah Ridder, Olivia Steeves and Eamon Naughton, who helped with footnotes.

# I. THE CHALLENGE OF INTEGRITY

·⊰✦⊱·

# CHAPTER 1

# THE DIVIDED LIFE
## A TALE OF TWO ADAMS

I grew up in the 1960s and 70s on the South Side of Chicago in a blue-collar neighborhood. One of the more dramatic moments of my teenage life occurred one Saturday night when four other teenagers from a local Catholic high school jumped me. The beating took place in front of the church our family attended.

The next morning, when our family went to Mass at that same church, I saw one of my assailants. Filled with self-righteous anger, I announced to my parents when I got home that I was never entering that church or any other Catholic Church—"so full of hypocrites"—again.

My mother, who was from Ireland, responded as only a mother to a teenage son would, "Michael, you know, there is always room for one more hypocrite."

This was not what I wanted to hear. I was the victim. I was the peace-loving kid. I was the person who wouldn't hurt a fly. But I was also, and unfortunately still am, a hypocrite.

My mother wanted me to learn a very important lesson in self-knowledge: namely, that when we think of sin or hypocrisy, our first thought should be of ourselves. G. K. Chesterton captured this lesson when he responded to a London newspaper's request for essays on the question, "What's wrong with the world?" He offered a startling two-word reply: "I am."

Of course, we would prefer to think of other people's failings—greedy business people, pompous professors, corrupt politicians, cliquey and self-absorbed teenagers, self-righteous clergy. Focusing on other people's sins instead of our own is a comfortable approach to life, since it demands little change from us. It allows us to keep our sins secret, private, and unacknowledged. But as Fr. Raniero Cantalamessa, the papal household preacher, once said, hypocrisy "is perhaps the most widespread human vice, and the least confessed."[1]

This is why, as Archbishop Charles Chaput explained, "Every other lens we use for understanding the human story, whether we choose economics or gender or Darwin or race or something else, will ultimately lie to us about

---

[1] Zenit, "First Lenten Sermon of Fr. Cantalamessa," March 11, 2007, https://zenit.org/articles/1st-lenten-sermon-of-father-cantalamessa/.

who we are."[2] These other lenses lie not because they do not offer insight, but because they fail to get to the roots of who we really are as created beings.

One of the great truths we need to discover is that there is a created order—one that has been given to us. We are not on this earth by mere chance. You and I are on a great adventure—an adventure that calls us to a shared good, a common good, and not merely a private one.

Yet, once we recognize this created order, this deep sense of transcendence, we experience the gap between who we have been created to be and who we actually are right now. This gap—what we call sin and hypocrisy—takes on multiple expressions, but one dimension that none of us escape is the temptation of the divided life.

As is true of most failings, we see the problem of a divided life more clearly in others than in ourselves. The Second Vatican Council describes the divided life as "the split between the faith which many profess and their daily lives." This split creates a false opposition between public and private spheres, faith and work, professional and religious life. The Council explains that this split and divide

[2] Archbishop Charles Chaput, "Archbishop Chaput on the Common Good," Catholic Online, April 2007, https://www.catholic.org/featured/headline.php?ID=4317&page=2.

"deserves to be counted among the more serious errors of our age."[3]

The problem of the divided life is a topic that creates great drama in movies. In the 2005 film *Cinderella Man*, it is captured with wonderful clarity in a dialogue between boxing promoter Jimmy Johnston and Joe Gould, the boxing manager for James Braddock (played by Russell Crowe), a onetime boxing champion making a comeback. Gould tells Johnston that he is "all heart" for promoting this comeback fight. Johnston sharply responds, "My heart's for my family, Joe, my brains . . . are for business, and this is business. You got me?" Gould responds, "Gotcha."

Johnston's response represents one of the most significant expressions of the divided modern life: there is a personal value system represented by the "heart" and a separate set of values for work represented by the "head." This compartmentalized view of life separates one's identity or role into distinct spheres of values, such that certain behaviors may be considered permissible in one realm but not in the other. At home, one expresses sympathy, compassion, and forgiveness, but at work everything is about calculation, efficiency, and utility.

---

[3]  Second Vatican Council, Pastoral Constitution on the Church in the Modern World *Gaudium et spes* (December 7, 1965), §43.

## ADAM I AND ADAM II: THE ACTIVE AND CONTEMPLATIVE LIFE

There are many reasons for the modern phenomenon of the divided life, but one very important root of the problem involves the relationship between the active and contemplative life. We were created both to work and to rest, both to be active and to be contemplative. These two dimensions of our lives are meant to inform each other as part of a deeper whole rather than exist as two modes of being that balance each other or effectively cancel each other out. For us to get a better grasp of this reality, we need to return to our origins, in particular, to the Book of Genesis, the first book of the Bible.

The Orthodox Jewish rabbi Joseph Soloveitchik explains that in Genesis there are not one, but two creation stories. He calls these two accounts "Adam I" and "Adam II."[4] For Soloveitchik, the reason for the two creation stories in Genesis is not simply that there happened to be two alternate traditions kicking around, but instead that these stories address the two essential dimensions of our humanity. To see these two accounts merely in terms of two narratives slapped together misses the point and can undermine the profound insights the Book of Genesis gives us.

These two creation stories represent a profound syn-

---

[4] Joseph Soloveitchik, *The Lonely Man of Faith* (New York: Three Leaves Press, 1965).

thesis of who we have been created to be. Unfortunately, we often find these "two Adams" in tension and alienated from each other, thus frustrating and disordering creation. Soloveitchik describes this tension as the great dilemma for the person of faith.

In the first creation story, we encounter Adam I, the active Adam, *homo faber*, "man the maker." Here we see humanity as a creative potency of invention and discovery that mirrors God's creative nature. Adam I wants to know *how* the cosmos functions. His goal is mastery over the world—a mastery he achieves by means of work, innovation, ingenuity, industriousness, and courage. Through scientific knowledge and technical application, the entrepreneur, the engineer, the farmer, the manager, and the tradesman carry out the command to "fill the earth and subdue it" (Gen 1:28).

Adam I is about mission. He ventures out into the world and produces change that makes the world a better place. He is committed to the successful production, distribution, and consumption of material and cultural goods. Adam I is a practically oriented achiever and problem solver. According to the insightful cultural commentator David Brooks, Adam I presents the "the career-oriented, ambitious side of our nature. Adam I is the external, resumé Adam. Adam I wants to build, create, produce, and discover things."[5] His participation in the divine creativity produces great achievements in the world.

We are created to labor as a bird is to fly. Adam I is acting in accordance with God's creative act. He is a co-creator with God, discovering creation's hidden riches and making them available and useful to others. Adam I reveals the "creative" endowment of being made in the image of God.

The second story of creation in Genesis gives us, in Adam II, a very different picture of humanity. Soloveitchik speaks of Adam II as *homo receptor*, "man the receiver," emphasizing the contemplative dimension of humanity. Adam II is placed in the garden to till and keep it (Gen 2:15). He seeks meaning not primarily in his achievements but in his received relationships with family, friends, and God, as well as in the experience of the natural world: sickness, death, love, suffering, and play.

Like Adam I, Adam II is intrigued by the cosmos, but the questions he asks are less about how and more about *why*. They are less practical and functional, and more philosophical and ultimately theological in nature. Adam II wants to know the purpose of creation, its meaning, and his role within it. He does not mathematize the world, but rather, as Soloveitchik puts it, "looks for the image of God

---

[5] David Brooks, *The Road to Character* (New York: Random House, 2015), xi–xii.

. . . in every beam of light, in every bud and blossom, in the morning breeze and the stillness of a starlit evening."[6] When Adam II looks at a rose, for example, he sees not only its parts, but its whole, where beauty is captured not through analysis but through awe, wonder, imagination, poetry, and praise.

Adam II is the protector of culture and the guardian of the "covenantal community," the relationships nurtured in cultural institutions such as marriage and family, religion, and education. Adam II nurtures and ensures connection to the cultural monuments of language, history, and tradition, realities that engage the fundamental events of our life—birth, death, love, suffering.

At the heart of Adam II is the *religious* person. While the word "religion" has a serious public image problem today, it can be good to be reminded that the root of the word comes from the Latin *religio*, which means *to reconnect*, to put us in touch with the deepest aspect of reality: God. That is why Adam II is a "praying man," both individually and communally. At the heart of prayer is the inner experience of self-surrender to God. In both its personal and liturgical forms, prayer centers around not *what I want*, but *what God wants from me*. The essence of prayer and worship is the sacrificial offering of oneself to God.

A simple chart that puts our two Adams side by side

---

[6] Soloveitchik, *The Lonely Man of Faith*, 22.

can help us to see the qualities of the active and contemplative life.

| Adam I | Adam II |
|---|---|
| Active | Contemplative |
| Labor | Leisure |
| Achievement | Reception |
| The How | The Why |
| Productive Communities | Covenantal Communities |
| Economy and Politics | Culture |
| Doing | Being |
| Dignity | Redemption |

## ADAM I'S ALIENATION OF ADAM II

These two Adams, both the active and receptive/contemplative, are within us, and it is only in their mutual penetration that we can become who we were created to be. While these two Adams ought to complement and fulfill each other, the world in which we live often puts them in tension. David Brooks captures these tensions succinctly:

> While Adam I wants to conquer the world, Adam II wants to obey a calling to serve the world. While Adam I is creative and savors his own accomplishments, Adam II sometimes renounces

worldly success and status for the sake of some sacred purpose. While Adam I asks how things work, Adam II ask why things exist, and what ultimately we are here for. While Adam I wants to venture forth, Adam II wants to return to his roots and savor the warmth of a family meal. While Adam I's motto is "success," Adam II experiences life as a moral drama. His motto is "Charity, love, and redemption."[7]

These tensions, which partly arise from our living in a world with limited time and resources, can easily create various alienations and disorders. Currently, the most common disorder is Adam I's alienation of Adam II. Adam I unhinges himself from Adam II, thereby marginalizing the qualities of receptivity, culture, prayer, and religion. Brooks again puts it well: "We live in a culture that nurtures Adam I, the external Adam, and neglects Adam II. We live in a society that encourages us to think about how to have a great career but leaves many of us inarticulate about how to cultivate the inner life."[8]

I have found this kind of alienation manifesting itself in my own life in many subtle ways. In one of those difficult but important discussions on the verge of arguments

[7] Brooks, *The Road to Character*, xii.
[8] Brooks, *The Road to Character*, xiii.

with my wife, she told me that my work often gets the best part of me, and she and the family get a worn out husband and father. Adam I has exhausted Adam II. The amount of energy and thought that goes into the goals and strategies of work creates an "Adam I only" identity. I often find that I turn personal conversations toward work, titles, and achievements far more than I should. I research and fixate on work issues, but all too easily neglect the deepening of my inner life by not having enough time for a Mass during the week or a retreat during the year.

This neglect of Adam II places achievement, the logic of the market, and economics above "receivement" and the logic of gift and culture. The question of the proper relationship between achieving and receiving will be a major theme throughout this book. A *market logic* holds the following precepts: "Input leads to output. Effort leads to reward. Practice makes perfect. Pursue self-interest. Maximize your utility. Impress the world."[9] When Adam I becomes unhinged from Adam II, these precepts give rise to a practice of utilitarianism and pragmatism. Work dominates life, progress is pursued for its own sake, and Adam I becomes a technological giant but spiritually small. He works more, prays less, and his humanity is disfigured.

Adam I starts to believe that his own unaided efforts are enough. He starts to believe that his talents and his

---

[9] Brooks, *The Road to Character*, xii.

sense of morality are enough to solve the problems that arise and to see him through to success. In taking this posture, he fails to recognize his moral and ethical indebtedness to Adam II. As Adam I increasingly dominates his personality, his mode of reasoning becomes more instrumental and technical, and his moral sense becomes unhinged from its deeper spiritual sources. Adam I unrealistically thinks that his moral bearings will remain the same even as he moves away from the religious dimensions of Adam II. He fails to recognize that as he becomes less religious and less receptive, he is undergoing a change; he is losing his relational and ethical sensibilities. And the tragedy is that often enough he does not know what is happening to himself.

Without Adam II, Adam I has lost his roots. He may still talk about the importance of ethics and values, but these values are merely instrumental to his own achievement: a means to an end rather than a way of being. His ethical principles look more like cut flowers than like a tree with roots. They look nice and have a pleasant aroma for a little while; but cut off from their transcendent sources, they wilt and begin to rot, and their pleasing aspect disappears. Adam I will speak about treating his employees well, or protecting the environment, or giving to the community, not because these actions are good in themselves, but only because they will make a difference for the bottom line, or because they have become the fad of the day and embracing them will make a good appearance. If such acts and attitudes are found to be unprofitable, or if the most recent fashion is actually unjust or coercive, deeper ethical concerns are thrown overboard.

Whatever his talents and his value, Adam I is always in desperate need of Adam II if he is not to go seriously astray. Adam I needs more than a logic of the market; he needs Adam II's *logic of the gift*, a contemplative outlook that receives the reality of the world—not as earned by him or his right to possess—but as a gift. The logic of gift is rooted in the family, where life is given. Above all, it is rooted in faith and the Church, where grace is given. It is planted deeply in those human institutions that connect people to one another far beyond the present and into the past and future.

Our work, which is our means of giving, must be characterized by a posture of receiving. Learning how to receive teaches us how to give. As the Book of Genesis tells us, we are made not only for work, but also for rest, and it is in rest and receptivity that our deepest reality is revealed. We need a posture of receiving informed by the receptivity of God's love for us. Otherwise, we will be unable to resist the temptation of only giving ourselves to achievements of measured and functional outcomes for personal success. While such achievements may bring momentary bursts of happiness or satisfaction, they will ultimately leave us divided from our deepest selves.

## CONCLUSION: BEYOND BALANCE

The divided life has been a serious problem throughout history. So thorny is the problem that Soloveitchik does not see how Adam I and Adam II can be reintegrated. In one sense he is right; we cannot reconcile Adam I and II. Christ can, however, through His grace, teaching, Word, and Sacraments. Christ is the new Adam, who redeems humans from their fragmentation and brings forth a new day, the Eighth Day, Sunday, which brings together heaven and earth. The Incarnation and the sacramental life that follows from it invite us into a deep unity of life, a unity that we can begin to experience even now before our final renewal in the eternal presence of God.

Yet while Christianity brings genuine hope for deeper integration, the danger for many Christians is a kind of naïve optimism about the therapeutic self. Too many Christians, lay and clergy alike, make glib claims such as, "I have integrity," and parrot the trite slogans of the culture, "I do what I say and say what I do," thinking that they have thereby solved the problem of Original Sin. The superficiality and lack of reflection in such an approach brings about a cheap integrity. Smug and self-righteous, such people are about as deep as a puddle. The temptation is present for all of us; we want a simple resolution, but what we really need is a rescue.

We prefer to take the easy route to dealing with the

problem of the divided life, so we use phrases such as "work/life balance" as though some sort of planned program will be able to solve this fundamental problem of the human condition. "Balance" has become one of those overused words in the workplace vocabulary. While it has its place, the "balance of work and faith" will often perpetuate, rather than confront and overcome, the divided life.

Balance is an attempt to manage something in a calculative way by weighing options and putting more on one side or the other of the scale. This is a very different matter from the task of integration, by which each element informs, corrects, and complements the other.

Integrating Adam I and Adam II does not mean giving our work lives a second-class status. Work is central to the practical life of goal-setting and decision-making and of personal and interpersonal achievement, from which springs our well-being as creatures who are by nature doers. This is why we speak so often of principled action, of the virtues, and of the common good, all of which point to the importance of the active life—the life of Adam I.

But our world has tended to entirely discount Adam II. It has been seduced by the idea—usually unexamined—that the achievements of Adam I alone can lead to deep satisfaction, happiness, and integrity. This is a serious error.

Thus, we come to the thesis of this book, which is

also a working principle for the whole of life: if we do not get rest or leisure right, we cannot get work right. If we have no place for Adam II, we will find that Adam I has become disfigured and dangerous. If we do not learn how to rightly integrate the posture of receiving—keeping Sunday as a day of rest, praying, living in covenanted relationship—then we will be wounded in our efforts at achievement: work, leadership, business, and production. Unless we confront this serious error of the divided life, especially in our professional formation, we will have little chance to resist the instrumental and dehumanizing forces so present in the workplace. We will find that our work has been reduced to nothing more than a "job" or a "career" with little meaning beyond itself, and that our rest has become superficial and lifeless. It is to these instrumental and utilitarian forces that we now turn.

---

CHAPTER 2

## SMALL WORK AND SHALLOW LEISURE

ON a different Saturday evening when I, at the age of sixteen, was walking out of the house, my father—who, like my mother, is from Ireland—said to me in his Irish brogue, "Michael, you be a good boy now." "Sure Dad," I replied, quickly adding that word favored by teenagers everywhere, "whatever." So he then went on to add a backup plan: "But if you can't be good, be *careful*." With some hesitation, I thought, "I can do that."

An unfortunate event happened to me that evening, however. I will spare you the details, but my dad eventually had to pick me up from a Chicago police station. He walked into the station and, as he looked at me, wryly revised his advice: "Michael, I think you better just be good!"

We live in a culture that has tended to lose sight of being good, fixating instead on being careful. For instance, we have:

- "designated drivers": safe and careful people who take home their drunk and stupid friends
- "safe sex," as if non-productive, disease-free intercourse replaces its unitive and procreative meaning
- educational pathways that fixate on good grades and test scores, checking all the necessary boxes to get to the next step, but in the process destroy the love of learning in a whole generation of students
- career strategies that calculate the effects of our actions in climbing the proverbial ladder of success but lose sight of good and meaningful work.

Business is lured in particular by this temptation to be *only* careful—what some have called a utilitarian mindset by which everything is evaluated on the basis of its immediate usefulness. Because business is rightly concerned about being practical and useful, this utility-driven mentality can subdue us into a false unity of life that over a lifetime creates a shallow and superficial existence.

If we were to live as if our faith mattered, if we were to be good beyond the fleeting slogans of our culture, we would ask ourselves some big questions—big enough to open our minds to see what is at stake and our hearts to embrace what should be loved. Here are three of these questions:

- *What am I working for?* To what am I giving myself in the work I do? Our work is too important to us to deprive ourselves of a serious answer. Yet a good answer will not come from within our work alone, since the dynamics of work do not provide enough depth to get to the heart of the matter. We need to ask a second question.

- *What am I resting in?* What am I receiving? The answer to our work will be found in our rest, our leisure—in what we receive. As the Book of Genesis tells us, we are made not only to work but also to rest.

- *What am I living for?* What is the meaning of my life? If we can put the prior two questions together such that they inform each other, we can get to the heart of the real meaning of our lives. The point is not simply to find a balance between work and rest, between the active and the contemplative life, but rather to participate in their proper integration.

We will spend the next two chapters examining these three questions. The answers we formulate will help us both to overcome the problem of a divided life and to build a good organization and business. In this chapter, we will focus on two versions of the relationship between work and leisure that tend to be the default views of our time. In the next chapter, we will articulate a vision of the active and contemplative life able to give us the capacity to live with integrity—with true integration.

## I. WORK AS A JOB, LEISURE AS AMUSEMENT

### The Job

For my friends who grew up with me in a blue-collar neighborhood on the South Side of Chicago, there is only one answer to the question "What am I working for?" that would not provoke a wearily cynical response: "Money." They would explain that work was just a "job" and that there was no sense in trying to get more out of it than it could give. Were I to suggest to them that work was a vocation, I would be met with the accusation that I was not engaging reality. "Mike, you have been too long in the ivory tower of the academy, and too sheltered from the real world."

My South Side friends might quote a fellow Chicago-an, the local newspaper columnist Mike Royko: "If work is so great why do they have to pay us to do it?" A sign in the kitchen at Al's Breakfast diner here in the Twin Cities neatly captures this attitude: "There's no fulfillment here." If you are looking for fulfillment, go somewhere else. You won't find it in the workplace.

It would be a mistake to think that this "just a job" attitude toward work is present only among blue-collar workers. Managers and professionals can have the same attitude as well. A lot of business education promotes a "money only" idea of work. Nearly every economics textbook tells us that we are self-interested utility maximizers. And just about every finance textbook says that the purpose of business is the maximization of shareholder value. While many businesses will speak of corporate social responsibility, philanthropy, sustainability, and business ethics, these so-called "values activities" are often seen as means to greater long-term profits—not as good ends in themselves.

Leaders who see their work as only a job tend to think of their companies in only bureaucratic and technocratic terms. They show themselves to be more concerned about being careful than about being good, and when they do speak of the good, it is merely as one more means of being careful.

Few of us desire to become bureaucrats; the word has a brittle sound to it. Yet if we see our work as only a job, we will lose sight of the deeper purposes of work and risk becoming mere bureaucrats. A common slogan of the business bureaucrat is "No margin, no mission." Most slogans have an element of truth to them; in this case the slogan rightly notes that if a business makes no profit, it will cease to exist. But the danger of this slogan is that bureaucratic leaders can get stuck on producing "margin" and never get around to articulating "mission." By creating systems whose sole focus is to measure margin, profit, efficiency, and productivity, such business leaders often have little time for a serious consideration of their mission.

Along with "No margin, no mission" comes the slogan "If it can't be measured, it can't be managed." Measurements are important. They tell us whether our actions are having an effect on a problem or goal. They give us indications of where things are heading. They can bring to light problems, trends, and opportunities.

But there is a downside to this rage for the measureable. The danger lies in thinking that our measurements can exhaust reality. We can start to believe that our metrics somehow take prudential judgment, and especially moral judgment, out of the equation. We increasingly discount and ignore faith, imagination, virtue, and most important of all, charity—serious matters that are not quantified easily and are in some cases simply immeasurable. The good accountant knows that the numbers he or she produces are indicators pointing to a larger reality. The numbers are not unimportant, but they only begin to tell the story. They do not exhaust it.

There is another problem that comes with relying too much on measurements. The more one measures a thing, the greater is the danger of driving the spirit out of what is being measured. We can thereby create organizations that have "form without spirit." I have encountered this dynamic in my teaching. The more you test your students, the more you grade them, and the more precision you get out of the grade, the more burdensome becomes the process for the student, until, finally, the love of learning is snuffed out. Grades are important, and standards are critical, but we can try to get more out of them than they can give.

So why do people look at work as a job? There are lots of reasons. One is that some jobs are designed so poorly and managed so bureaucratically that the only possible good one can get from them is money. But there is a cultural reason why we look at work as a job, one that is connected to how we look at our *rest*.

## Leisure as Amusement

So deeply ingrained in our current culture is the obsession with entertainment that we have begun to think that it is natural to human life. We have begun to think that things have always been this way, but the amount of time and energy that we spend on entertainment is in fact unique to modern societies. We love to be amused. Increasingly, we view our non-work time in terms of entertainment. The consequences of this mindset are evident among average salaries. Many of the highest paid people in our culture are entertainers. There are, of course, lots of starving actors, musicians, and athletes, but the American entertainment industry is a huge part of the economy and one of our largest exporters.

There are many reasons for the modern obsession

with entertainment, but one important dynamic seems to be our need for escape and distraction. In his song "The Piano Man," Billy Joel captures this: "Cause he knows that it's me they've been coming to see to forget about life for a while." Leisure, for much of history, was time set aside for remembering the most important things, for rediscovering ourselves and thinking about who we ought to be. But modernly, as Jacques Ellul wrote, leisure has become "the moment when amusements succeed to the maximum in making [us] . . . forget."[1] Rather than discovering and penetrating the meaning and mystery of our lives, modern leisure amuses us into escaping from our lives.

The very word "amusement" reveals a deeper level of our modern problem. The word comes from the Muses, Greek goddesses who were divine patrons of the liberal arts. The Muses were sources of refreshment and inspiration to those under their influence, stirring up the intelligence and the imagination—whatever helped humans to remember who they were and to understand the world. The word a-musement means a denial of the influence of the muses. In Greek, to put an "a" in front of the world implies a lack of whatever the word means. Thus, to be a theist is to believe in God, whereas to be an *a*theist is to deny God's existence. Wiktionary defines amuse as "to stare stupidly" at something.[2]

---

[1] Jacques Ellul, "Reflections on Leisure," *Interplay* 54 (December 1967).
[2] "Amuse," Wiktionary: The Free Dictionary (website), updated September 30, 2018, https://en.wiktionary.org/wiki/amuse.

(This is my wife's description of me as I watch television.)

Paradoxically, when leisure is reduced to amusement it fails to give us rest; we become restless. After a bout of binging on Netflix or video games we find ourselves dis-eased, or, what has become the worst state possible, bored. Just as too much sleep makes us tired, sluggish, and apathetic, so also too much entertainment makes us anxious. How sad it is, then, that amusement forms of leisure are our default mode. As soon as we have a moment of free time we turn on the TV or go to the smartphone, thinking to find refreshment; and when we are finished, we feel anxious, bored, or vaguely guilty, knowing that we should have been doing something else.

Our advertising system has exploited this temptation to amusement. A couple of years ago I saw an ad for a hotel chain touting a weekend getaway. A couple in a swimming pool were looking at each other in a rather non-platonic fashion with the caption, "Where your body checks in and your mind checks out." The ad captured in both an image and a phrase the modern form of leisure. It described the weekend as a time to flee reality, rather than a time to penetrate it more authentically. The inhuman harshness of the economic grind of work gives an added impetus to this form of seeking relief.

Whether it be weekend getaways, malls and shopping, casinos, spas, television, movies, sports, concerts, amusement parks, cruises, internet, video games, or strip joints, we are constantly seeking a way to escape, to "veg out," to flee our current existence in gratifying illusions. We make a weekend jaunt to Las Vegas and delude ourselves that "what happens in Vegas, stays in Vegas." The only thing that really stays in Vegas is our money. All of our actions and their consequences come right back with us on the plane.

## Integration: Consumerism

When work has been reduced to a job—and rest or leisure to amusement—our vision of the world starts to gel under the banner of consumerism. By this lens we grow more concerned about what we *have* and less concerned about what we *become* in having. When leisure is predominately restricted to entertainment and consumption, it fails to provide the moral and spiritual resources necessary to offer a robust notion of the good. Shaped by this attenuated leisure, we settle in for a conventional and thin description of the good that has neither the capacity to inspire greatness nor the resources to overcome our impulses toward unending consumption.

## II. WORK AS CAREER, LEISURE AS UTILITY

### Work as Career

Unlike those in a "job," who tend to see work only as a means to an economic end, careerists experience work as a source of self-esteem, creativity, and personal satisfaction.

Their work involves an application of their talents and abilities to solve problems and contribute to solutions. They feel a high degree of control and competence in what they do.

Careerists are not so much money-mad as they are goal-oriented.[3] In many respects, the careerist reflects the very etymology of the name: *car*eer. Both "career" and "car" refer to movement, and increasingly a private way of movement, in order to achieve particular goals. The car, one's "*auto*-mobile," or self-driven vehicle, lets a person travel alone in whatever direction that person desires. In similar terms, the careerist calculates his travels not in public but in private terms. Like the privacy of a car, the careerist is interested in whatever goals—whether education, contacts, money, skill, or power—are necessary to get from here to there.[4]

So why do people look at work as a career? Again, there are lots of reasons, but to understand the process better, let's look at another conception of rest or leisure—not as a means of amusement, but rather of utility.

## Leisure as Utility

The dominance of work in our culture has tended to en-

---

[3] David Brooks, "The Organization Kid," *The Atlantic Monthly* (April 2001): 40–54.

[4] William May, "The Beleaguered Rulers: The Public Obligation of the Professional," *Kennedy Institute of Ethics Journal* 2 (1992): 31.

croach upon our view of rest or leisure such that we increasingly view our leisure as only a means to serve work. We can see this dynamic present in our view of education.

Increasingly, education is justified only by its *instrumental* and useful value to a hoped-for career. As my students will complain, "Dr. Naughton, like, why do I have to take theology, or philosophy, or art? Like, what will it do for my career?" I respond by explaining to them that the word for leisure comes from the Latin "*scola*," from which we also get our words "school" and "scholar"; school is leisure. With a pause of awkward silence, they respond, "Ah, no, I don't think so, Dr. Naughton."

Education has so distanced itself from leisure that the connection between the two is almost laughable. But the Greeks, Romans, and Christians saw the importance of the connection for more than two thousand years. The notion of the liberal arts, at the heart of the origin and development of universities, involves seeing all things in relation, seeing the place of God in His relation to all reality and the world as a sacred creation in which God is ever at work.

John Henry Newman, whose book *The Idea of a University* remains one of the most influential writings on education we have, held that an education focused only on being useful runs into the inevitable question: Useful for what? It is precisely the "what" that raises the question of the "good." Can usefulness and utility provide their own criteria of goodness? If education is seen as the means to increase the economic goods of profit, efficiency, and productivity, the nagging question remains: Profits for what? Efficiency for what?

Newman coined a principle that is simple and straightforward: "The good is always useful, but the useful is not always good."[5] It is precisely here that we have witnessed some major world disorders—both economic and geopolitical—caused, at least in part, by a university education that failed to connect the professional and the liberal aspects of education, that has pursued the useful at the expense of the good. Noted philosopher Alasdair MacIntyre has argued that these disorders "have been brought about by some of the most distinguished graduates of some of the most distinguished universities in the world."[6]

MacIntyre gives the following events and developments as examples: the Vietnam and Iraq Wars, the American policy toward Iran that produced the Iranian Hostage Crisis, and the 2008 financial crisis. MacIntyre's point is well-taken: when we prepare graduates to simply "be careful," to be specialists in their field alone, to think instrumentally with no philosophical or theological

---

[5] John Henry Newman, *The Idea of a University* (Lexington, KY: Forgotten Books, 2012), discourse 7, no. 5.
[6] Alasdair MacIntyre, "The Very Idea of a University: Aristotle, Newman, and Us," *British Journal of Educational Studies* 57, no. 4 (December, 2009): 361.

root system, the result is a narrow education that creates specialists without spirit, politicians without heart, and businesspeople without principle, all of which lead to the failure to know and bring about the good.

Newman helps us to see that once a theological vision or formation within an education is removed, the professions increasingly become secularized and "careerized" and lose the capacity not only to examine, but even to ask, important questions about what makes the useful good. Universities often tout slogans about training students to be "critical thinkers" so that they can think "for themselves." Yet without any substantive notion of the good, students are only one step away from thinking only *of themselves.*

## INTEGRATION: CAREERISM

When we view our work as a career and rest or leisure in terms of utility, we increasingly perceive our identity as only tied to our achievements. This is careerism, the mindset in which we are more concerned about what we achieve than about who we have become in achieving.

Lee Iaccoca famously engineered one of the most significant turnarounds in American business when he took the Chrysler Corporation out of bankruptcy in the 1980s. In the early 90s, Iaccoca retired. Three years later, he was on the cover of the *Fortune* magazine with the caption, "How I Flunked Retirement." This icon of American industry, who rescued a major auto company, explained that his three years of retirement were more stressful than his forty-seven years in the auto business. He was an economic giant at work, but he was a spiritual dwarf in retirement. He knew who he was at work, but outside of the corporation he was simply at sea. No amount of achievement can justify a broken soul. One can only admire Iacocca for being so honest about it to the public.

## CONCLUSION

The problem we have been discussing, the moral and spiritual task of integrating work and leisure, can be best described as the "two-ditch" problem. Every road has not one ditch but two—one on either side. As regards to work, the two ditches that we can fall into come from either undervaluing or overvaluing our work and its place in our lives.

On one side of us is the "job ditch" of undervaluing ourselves in our work. Falling into this ditch, we expect too little out of our work and we fail to recognize how important it is for our human formation. An important insight from the Catholic social tradition as it relates to the work deals with what Pope John Paul II called the *subjective dimension* of work. This dimension helps us to see that when we act, we not only affect and change objects outside of ourselves, but more profoundly, we change our very selves.

On the other side of the road is the "career ditch," in which we overinvest ourselves in work and expect more from it than it can give. When we fall into this ditch, we expect our career to define us, to provide us with a meaningful identity. The result is an inner void and a confused sense of identity. Philosopher Josef Pieper has described the identity problem of the careerist as *acedia*, a "deep-seated lack of calm which makes leisure impossible." Acedia is a restlessness of spirit that means, a "despairing refusal to be oneself."[7]

Acedia is considered one of the seven capital sins. Unfortunately, because it is often translated as "slothful" or "lazy," it is often thought that acedia can be overcome by diligence and more work. But more work or more intensive work is often the last thing that careerists need if they are to confront their acedia. There is a lazy or slothful component to this vice, but it is principally found in a spiritual and not physical laziness. Often, the careerist becomes a workaholic, precisely to avoid the rest necessary to be oneself.

These two "ditches," mistaken views of work and their corresponding connections to leisure, do great damage to our capacity to live with integrity. What we need instead is a faith-filled response to our work and our rest, a response that touches the deepest impulse of our humanity, one that Pope Benedict XVI called the "logic of gift."

---

[7]  See Josef Pieper, *Leisure: The Basis of Culture* (South Bend: St. Augustine's Press, 1998), 28. Pieper is quoting philosopher Søren Kierkegaard.

·❖·

CHAPTER 3

# THE LOGIC OF GIFT
## THE CALL TO GIVE AND RECEIVE

I had the opportunity to meet Mother Teresa twice in my life. One of these times was in 1995, when I gave a talk at the Indian Institute of Management in Calcutta. My host, who was Hindu, knew I was Catholic and arranged the meeting. Mother Teresa asked us questions about our lives and our work. She also talked about her work and, in particular, her desire to open a house in China. She was asked once, "Why China?" and she responded, "My great desire is to meet anybody who has nobody."

As we were leaving, Mother Teresa, with a grin on her face, said to us, "I want to give you my business card." There was no email, phone number, or title on the card, but only the following lines:

The fruit of SILENCE is Prayer

The fruit of PRAYER is Faith

The fruit of FAITH is Love

The fruit of LOVE is Service

The fruit of SERVICE is Peace

What made Mother Teresa such a beautiful woman was her openness to God. For it was Christ who chose her. She began her days by following the advice on her business card: turning to God in interior *silence* that turned to powerful *prayer*, that gave her great *faith* and an extraordinary capacity to *love* and *serve* others, not once in a while but on a habitual basis, with a deep *peace* that she was to be right where she was and not anywhere else.

Mother Teresa's witness, along with the witness of many good holy men and women throughout history, confronts a particular temptation that we face in modern life, namely, that we lose touch with God's call. We are His chosen ones, but we often forget or don't believe it. Instead, we focus only on our own choices. We have, unfortunately, come to see personal choice, and not the content of that choice, as of the highest value. Mother Teresa's business card reminds us that our choices only make sense in terms of what we are chosen for.

Without a deep sense of "being chosen," in the recognition that God has a plan for each one of us, our choices will not free us, but rather will empty us of any meaning or significance. When we focus on our choice with the trite and all-too-common phrase "We all need to make our own choices," we fall into a pit that we can't get out of.

This pit is captured by the English novelist and poet D. H. Lawrence, who wrote: "Men are not free when they are doing just what they like. The moment you can do just what you like, there is nothing you care about doing."[1] We are most free when we are obeying the deep, inward voice of God's call—not when we are escaping to some undefined "wild west." It is the truth that sets us free, a truth that is most profoundly expressed in the intimate call that God has given us. In the gifts we have received from Him and the use we put them to, we both make the world a better place and become who we were created to be.

In a career- and consumer-oriented world, too often we can see work merely in terms of personal preferences, of our own passions and dreams, of our choices. This individualistic orientation (although, ironically, highly conformist) sees the world not as an integrated order, created and given by the Creator, with its own *logic of gift*, but rather as a collection of raw material at humanity's disposal—to be manipulated according to human decisions and abilities

---

[1] D. H. Lawrence, *Studies in Classic American Literature* (New York: Penguin, 1923), 12–13.

only within the limits of extrinsic legal rules.

In contrast to the individualism inherent in the notion of a "job" or a "career," we long to discover the truth that our work is not only about our discrete and arbitrary choices, but instead depends on a choice to participate in a received, created order expressed in terms of the logic of gift. Because gift is at the heart of this stance, it is a call that is not *achieved* but *received*, not accomplished but accepted.

At the heart of this call, then, is not a theory or ethic that one can create or master, but rather a Person whose deep and inexhaustible love can only be received as grace, as a gift that we have not earned. As expressed on Mother Teresa's business card, it is this orientation toward silence, prayer, faith, love, service, and peace that has the capacity to transform us and the communities in which we live.

We are looking, then, for an integrated dynamic of receiving and giving, of rest and work, of contemplation and action. Hans Urs von Balthasar captures this dynamic when he speaks about St. Thomas Aquinas. "Thomas was fully conscious of this paradox of the creature, namely, that the more it is receptive to God, the more it participates in his activity, so that, as the power of contemplation increases, so does that of action." We can therefore say, "Action occurs not... to the detriment of contemplation, but as its fulfillment."[2]

---

[2] Hans Urs von Balthasar, *Explorations in Theology*, vol. I, *The Word Made Flesh* (San Francisco: Ignatius Press, 1989), 234.

# WORK: VOCATION OF THE ACTIVE LIFE

"Vocation" comes from the Latin *vocare*, "to call." In Greek, "vocation" comes from the root *klesis*, which is also the root of the New Testament word for Church, *ekklesia*. These two meanings of vocation—a personal call and a community in which this call is nurtured, discerned, and realized—mark the two essential dimensions of a vocation. These personal and communal dimensions inform the vocation of work.

On the personal level of vocation, we experience a deep and particular sense that we are made for something, that we are called to be someone. John Henry Newman once put it this way: "God created me to do Him some definite service; He has committed some work to me which He has not committed to another. . . . He has not created me for naught. I shall do good; I shall do His work."[3] Newman captures this deep sense that we are at our best not when we are calculating, scheming, or fixated on our self-interest, but when we are giving ourselves to others. As the Second Vatican Council put it, a person "cannot fully find himself except through a sincere gift of himself."[4] This notion of gift reveals our very nature as human persons.

[3] John Henry Newman, *Meditations and Devotions of the Late Cardinal Newman* (New York: Longmans, Green, and Co., 1900), 301.
[4] Second Vatican Council, *Gaudium et spes*, §24.

According to this logic of gift, we find ourselves asking different questions: not only "What do I want from life?" but also "What does life want from me?" and "What does God want from me?" These questions remove us from the center of our lives and create room for social and transcendent realities: the call is bigger than I am, although it includes me. Within the logic of gift, we do not create our lives; instead, we are called and summoned by life. The important answers to our deepest questions are found not only inside but also outside ourselves. Vocational discernment is never merely a form of naval gazing, and this fact brings us to the second aspect of our vocation.

Our second call is to a state of life, to a particular way of belonging. In the Catholic tradition, we speak of three states of life: lay, priestly, and religious. To look again at the Greek word *ekklesia*, the root "*ek*" means "out of" and, as we have seen, the root "*klesis*" means "calling." *Ekklesia* thus refers to the assembly that has been called out. The Church plays an important role as a mediator in the discernment of our state of life, especially for those who believe they are called to the priestly and religious life. The Church also helps the laity discern the vocation to single life or marriage.

These three states of life fostered by the Church are distinct but complementary. When these states are strongly embraced, the Church is vibrant and effective, but if any of them lose their hold within the Church, its life and work falter. We might think of the three states of life as three legs of a stool. Each leg supports the life of the Church in a particular way that strengthens the other; if one weakens the stool, eventually the stool becomes unstable.

The idea of complementarity resists notions of competition, imitation, status, superiority, exclusive hierarchy, or egalitarianism. For example, most priests and religious come from well-formed and holy families, and priests and religious play an important role in forming and equipping the laity to become holy and to transform the temporal (secular) order so that all realms of human endeavor may properly serve the human person. We see this in the lives of many saints of the Church, such as Mother Teresa, Benedict of Nursia, Francis of Assisi, Teresa of Lisieux, and Ignatius of Loyola. Their lives of dedicated consecration inspire the Church and the laity to live the Gospel in the world.

A third aspect of our vocation, which is embedded and informed by the two prior aspects, is the summons to a particular *way* of working. This does not necessarily mean that we are called to a very specific form of work, although it may. But if we are not able to find work that seems to fit our calling, or if we get laid off, it does not mean our vocation is on hold. No matter what kind of work we do, we are called to give ourselves to it.

A powerful story that reveals this gifted character of life, this law of gift, is found in Lewis Hyde's book *The Gift*, in which he speaks of the "gift economy." Hyde recounts that when Native Americans encountered Puritans in their first set of gift encounters, they were baffled by the Puritans' possessiveness over gifts given them.[5] The Native Americans expected their English visitors to give their gifts so as to keep them in circulation. This idea of setting gifts in motion equally baffled the English newcomers, who characterized Native Americans with the derogatory term "Indian givers."

What the Native Americans understood is that there is a natural law governing gifts: when a gift is not shared, it corrupts the holder. The one who makes the gift an occasion for selfish hoarding, who fails to put the gift in motion, becomes corrupted by the gift itself. It is the law of the gift. There is a natural and even divine law of sorts that "we actually become, eternally, what we have given ourselves to."[6] But the more we keep our gifts for ourselves, the more we become broken, lonely, and corrupted.

While most of us probably do not think that we work only for ourselves, there are subtle ways in which our gifts

[5] See Lewis Hyde, *The Gift: Imagination and the Erotic Life of Property* (New York: Random House, 1983), chap. 1.
[6] John F. Kavanaugh, "Last Words," *America: The Jesuit Review,* January 2002, 23.

can turn on us. I often find that I am most connected to my work, my family, my church, and my community when I am giving to something larger than myself. Yet I also find that the longer I give to a certain place or project, the more my giving can turn into a calculation with an interior price.

I have been at my university for over twenty-five years and have prided myself on waking up early almost every morning, working on articles, books, and other projects such as this one. In many of those works, I have collaborated with colleagues at St. Thomas, at other universities, and with Church and business leaders. The fruit of this work has been a project we call Catholic Studies. Almost invariably, however, in the midst of my labor, I would find myself comparing my efforts to those of my colleagues. Then would come my internal whining spirit: Why I am doing sixty, seventy, or eighty percent of the work here? Why am I the one making all the sacrifices? Why aren't the others pulling their load?

My "giving" would thus often lead to a form of victimization, which would be followed by resentment, cynicism, or anger. It was all quite subtle. I hardly noticed the gradual development of these attitudes, but, though subtle, the process was very real. My self-imposed martyrdom was not only neutralizing the potency of what I was giving, but actually turning my gift into a form of self-aggrandizement. I would "do more than my fair share" with a chip on my shoulder. I did my duty, but without spirit and under a love that was growing cold.

This is why the Latin phrase *nemo dat quod non habet*, "no one gives what he does not have," is so critical to our discussion. Whoever we are and whatever we do—whether CEO, pope, entrepreneur, mother, father, professor, or plumber—our work by itself will exhaust us. We need to receive what we do not have. And we need to constantly rediscover the gifts that have been given to us and confess the ways we have misused and disordered them. If we are to give rightly, we need to learn to receive rightly. And this brings us to the importance of leisure as contemplation.

## LEISURE: CONTEMPLATION AS RECEPTIVITY

The person "comes in the profoundest sense to himself not through what he does but through what he accepts," not through what he achieves but what he receives.[7] When we speak of acceptance, of receptivity, of leisure and rest, we need to recognize how different it is from our work and our accomplishments. Its structure is not an "achievement" on my part, but a "receivement," wherein I lay myself bare to accept what God wants of me.

This receptivity creates a contemplative outlook that does "not presume to take possession of reality but instead

[7] Joseph Cardinal Ratzinger, *Introduction to Christianity* (San Francisco: Ignatius Press, 2004), 267.

accepts it as a gift, discovering in all things the reflection of the Creator and seeing in every person his living image."[8] It is a receptivity that is ever new, unpredictable, and never settled, and it has the capacity to surprise us, to produce wonder along with the fear that we might need to change our ways of thought and action.[9]

Times of prayer in the morning, attendance at Mass, or a short prayer before a meeting are often not earth-shattering moments, but they gradually form a habit of openness to our place in creation. They can help us to be prepared for sickness, the acceptance of criticism and failure, the death of a loved one so that these difficult experiences lead us not to be bitter but better. Over a life, these moments can bring us profound growth in who we were created to be.

We are in great need of habits of receptivity, leisure and rest that root us in a contemplative life and enable us to give of ourselves in our active lives. There are three important habits of leisure that Christianity, along with other religious traditions, has fostered:

- The habit of silence: daily silence where our emotional tapes that have been playing for years can cease and where we can hear again

---

[8] John Paul II, Encyclical Letter on the Value and Inviolability of Human Life *Evangelium vitae* (March 25, 1995), §83.

[9] Hans Urs von Balthasar, *Prayer* (New York: Paulist Press, 1967), 20.

the wisdom that "deafens every fool."

- The habit of celebration: a weekly Sabbath where, as Abraham Heschel has put it, "the goal is not to have but to be, not to own but to give, not to control but to share, not to subdue but to be in accord."[10]

- The habit of charity: going to the margins to be with those who are unproductive, who lack power, but who have another sort of power over us, a power, like little else, that confronts who we really are.

Authentic leisure requires the humility to recognize that there are certain things in life that can only be received. We must stop our work and let ourselves be worked upon.

These habits of rest and leisure are difficult for us to receive, however, as we have been brought up on a heavy dose of individualism, consumerism, careerism, and athleticism that discount the importance of receptivity. It is precisely because of our refusal to receive that we find ourselves in so much trouble. When we take by force those things that should only be received, we violate the divine image within us. This refusal to receive is found in our origins, in the story of the fall of Adam and Eve, when God commanded them not to eat "of the tree of

---

[10] Abraham Joshua Heschel, *The Sabbath: Its Meaning for Modern Man* (New York: Farrar, 2005), 3.

knowledge of good and evil" (Gen 2:16–17). The moral law is given to us by God. We cannot take it as our own, manipulate it, or create it; we can only accept and embrace it.[11] When we take and achieve rather than accept and receive, as we should be doing, we distort our place within God's order, and our actions increasingly become characterized by an alienation that divides us both within ourselves and from others.

The philosopher Friedrich Nietzsche excelled in sketching the portrait of the person who cannot receive. His "noble man" or "superman" is one who regards "*himself* as determining values . . . he *creates values.*"[12] This notion of the person as essentially creative, active, and constructive not only distorts our place within the cosmos, but it overrates the role of work. This is why leisure as contemplation and receptivity must have a certain primacy.

## INTEGRITY: BECOMING WHOLE

When we start seeing our work as a vocation and our rest as contemplation, we begin to have the resources not simply for balance but for genuine integration, for becoming contemplative practitioners. Once we experience what it means to be receivers of creation, redemption, and grace,

---

[11] John Paul II, Encyclical Letter *Veritatis splendor* (August 6, 1993), §§35–7.

[12] Friedrich Nietzsche, *Beyond Good and Evil: Prelude to a Philosophy of the Future* (Oxford: Oxford University Press, 1998), 154.

then our doing and having can be given in the way they have been received.[13]

As we grow in our ability to integrate the active and contemplative aspects of life, we increasingly become people of integrity. The two etymological meanings of the word "integrity" can help us see what is at stake. In the first meaning, integrity comes from the Latin *integritas*, from which the word "integer," or whole number, is derived. The second meaning of integrity relates to being untouched, innocent, or pure. It is derived from the negating prefix *in-* combined with the verb *tangere* (to touch), conveying the idea that a person of integrity is someone who is un-touched, un-impaired, or un-blemished.[14] Thus, we can imagine what it means to be a person of integrity. Because of our fallen state, we are internally divided and are in need of becoming whole; we are blemished and corrupted and need to be purified.

By retrieving these two etymological roots of integrity (*integritas*, meaning "wholeness" and *in-tangere*, meaning "untouched" and "innocence"), we touch on the *being* of the person. To become whole and purified, to be restored to what we have lost, we need to participate in the dy-

---

[13] David Schindler, "Christology and the *Imago dei*: Interpreting *Gaudium et spes*," *Communio* 23 (Spring 1996): 179. See also Herbert Alphonso, *The Personal Vocation* (Rome: Centrum Ignatianum Spiritualitatis, 1990), 37.

[14] Margaret E. Mohrmann, "Integrity: *Integritas, Innocentia, Simplicitas*," *Journal of the Society of Christian Ethics* 24 no. 2, (2004): 25–37.

namic between receiving and giving defined by the *logic of gift*. Benedict explains that "charity is love received and given."[15] What is received is often profoundly discovered in the contemplative life, and what is given is often profoundly expressed in our active lives. This receiving and giving is like the inhaling and exhaling of life.

Gaining the integrity we seek is a tall order. Work as a job or career and leisure as amusement or utility do not have the resources to move us toward such integrity. They leave us divided, exhausted, and small. Of course, work is a job: we do work for money. There is nothing wrong with wanting to live better. And there is nothing wrong with work as a career. People who climb the so-called corporate ladder are often invited to take on greater responsibilities because their hard work and talent warrant it. The problem with the job and career approach is that it is simply too small for the human spirit. As Augustine writes in his *Confessions*, "The house of my soul is too small for you to come to it. May it be enlarged by you."[16] Our view of work can become so small that it is hard for God to enter, or better put, we can prevent God from entering.

The next four chapters will explore an *enlarged* vision of work in light of the logic of gift mediated by the social teachings of the Church. The business leader has been

---

[15] Benedict XVI, Encyclical Letter on Integral Human Development in Charity and Truth *Caritas in veritate* (June 29, 2009), §5.

[16] Augustine, *Confessions* (Oxford: Oxford University Press, 1991), 6.

given much, and therefore, much is expected of him. This logic of gift articulates the good that business does as an institution (chapter four). The vocation of the business leader is to build up the common good of the organization by ordering the goods of the business: good goods, good work, and good wealth (chapters five, six, and seven). These chapters elaborate on what we mean by the vocation of the business leader.

# II. LABOR

# CHAPTER 4

# THE PURPOSE OF BUSINESS
## DEFINING THE GOOD THAT BUSINESS DOES

FOR the last several years I have served as the chair of the board of directors for Reell Precision Manufacturing, a global producer of torque solutions for a variety of industries with offices and plants in the US, Netherlands, and China. The founders of the company are three men of faith who started their careers as engineers at the 3M company. Early on, they began to set the tone for what kind of business Reell would be. In a welcoming message to new coworkers, they started to define the *purpose* of the company in the following way:

> We do not define profits as the *purpose* of the company, but we do recognize that reasonable profitability is necessary to continue in business and to reach our full potential. We see profits in

much the same way that you could view food in your personal life. You probably do not define food or eating as the *purpose* of your life, but recognize that it is essential to maintain your health and strength so you can realize your real *purpose*.[1]

The founders of Reell recognized that if the pursuit of profits was not taken seriously, the business would soon collapse. They also recognized, however, that a healthy business should order profit to something larger than itself. Profit is a means, not an end. It makes a wonderful servant but a lousy master.

We cheapen business when we see it only in terms of making profits. Yet, this narrowing of purpose is not only a problem for business. Other institutions face the tendency to reduce themselves to one limited good: universities to career credentialing, religion to emotive experience, and marriage to sentiment between autonomous individuals. When we "thin out" institutions, reducing them from a vibrant set of integrated goods to one instrumental or emotive good, they become ineffective in serving the *common* good.

Thus, although many of our institutions have grown in size, they have shrunk in purpose. Some of our institutions have become small spaces both morally and spiritu-

[1] Kenneth E. Goodpaster and Laura L. Nash, *Policies and Persons*, 3rd ed. (New York: McGraw-Hill, 1998), 135–150 (emphasis added).

ally. They serve themselves rather than being committed to goods that serve a larger reality. When marriage, for example, is only about the preferences of the individuals, it begins to suffocate. When a business is geared simply to maximizing its own capital base, it eventually loses the capacity to know when to sacrifice short-term profits for something larger.

We need to think and act *institutionally*.[2] In a highly individualistic culture such as ours, this is a great challenge. We often don't think of our lives as moving from one institution to another, but they do. We are born into our families, formed by our various religions, educated in schools; we are healed at hospitals; we work for corporations, volunteer in organizations, and obey laws. Family, religion, schools, corporations, health care systems, volunteer organizations, and the state are all institutions, and we both shape these institutions and are shaped by them.

If we are to think institutionally, we cannot compartmentalize the institution of business from our other institutions—especially family and religion. We need to see the organic connection of business to the larger society and, in particular, to other societal institutions, if business is to be meaningful as well as legitimate.

[2] There are two important books that inform this chapter: Hugh Heclo, *On Thinking Institutionally* (Boulder, CO: Paradigm Publishers, 2008), 101; and Habiger Institute for Catholic Leadership, *True Leadership* (Providence, RI: Cluny Media, 2018).

We increasingly think about our institutions in a negative light, and we have good reason. Headlines on their moral decline abound: corporate financial misconduct, clerical sexual abuse, university insularity and political correctness, media bias, governmental corruption, military torture, police violence. The list goes on. We are wryly amused by Dilbert, one of the most popular comic strips addressing the moral and spiritual emptiness of the modern corporation. More and more we don't trust our institutions or their leaders. We see short-term actors who think and act only to get elected, sell stories, meet quarterly targets, get published, and so forth.

Not only do we mistrust institutions, we believe that we can be happy without them. But this is not the case. Studies indicate that those involved in various institutions, such as family, religion, work, or volunteer organizations, are happier than those who are not. One particular data point is revealing. Since 2000, suicide has risen steadily with a particular sharp rise among middle-aged men. The reasons for suicides are complicated and varied—anything from mental health, depression, or drugs—but there is a strong and obvious link between suicide and weakened institutional bonds. Ross Douthat points to "what we've seen happen lately among the middle-aged male population, whose suicide rates have climbed the fastest: a retreat from family obligations, from civic and religious participation, and from full-time paying work."[3] We are social by nature—institutional animals—and when we break away from our nature and our institutions, we pay a significant price.

In every age, institutional decline and corruption occurs, and in every age, we are called to renew and reform our institutions. Our age is no different. Our institutions have suffered damage, and one reason for this is that we have cheapened them by underestimating and disordering the goods they are designed to promote. As harsh as it may sound, we have become institutional parasites. We have benefited from the moral and spiritual institutional capital built up over many decades. We borrow from it, but we give nothing back.

Part of our vocation involves cultivating a mode of institutional thinking that can bring us to a richer understanding of the goods institutions create, promote, and protect. We need to see our lives through institutions, as well as to understand ourselves as builders of institutions.

For business, this ability to think institutionally requires two important thought processes. The first is cultural thinking. What kind of institution is business, and how is it connected to other institutions, especially those cultural institutions that gives us the roots of meaning and purpose? The second is business thinking: What is the good

---

[3] Ross Douthat, "All the Lonely People," *The New York Times*, May 18, 2013, Sunday Review, https://www.nytimes.com/2013/05/19/opinion/sunday/douthat-loneliness-and-suicide.html.

that business does as a business? What are the actual goods of business? And how do we order these goods to the common good? These two ways of thinking will prepare us to address the practical tensions and troubles as well as the joys and successes of running businesses and organizations.

## I. CULTURAL THINKING: GETTING TO THE ROOTS OF THINGS

Business has become an increasingly important institution in modern society in terms of its impact on the larger culture and in terms of its actual numbers. When we speak about business, we sometimes think too narrowly and only consider large multinational corporations. But business institutions are highly diverse, including family businesses, social businesses, cooperatives, partnerships, small entrepreneurial start-ups, and employee-owned businesses. While there are huge businesses that have revenues larger than some countries, most are small.

Take the US, for example. There are an estimated twenty-seven million businesses in America, most of which are small. Only 18,500 of these firms have five hundred or more employees. Approximately nineteen million are sole proprietorships, five million are family businesses, two million are partnerships, twenty-one thousand are cooperatives, eleven thousand are Employee Stock Ownership Plans, and six thousand are publicly traded corporations. We are a country of business institutions.

Yet, despite the size and importance of business in our world, business is not meant to be the place where we find meaning at the deepest level. Let's be clear: there is great meaning in business, but our deepest relationships and loyalty take place somewhere else. In other words, in terms of meaning and relationship, business—and the state, for that matter—are not primary institutions but secondary ones.[4] This distinction is important.

When we speak of "primary institutions," we refer to a "primacy" of meaning. Family and religion are primary institutions. Business, the state, educational institutions, and health care institutions are all secondary institutions. Secondary here does not mean unimportant or marginal. Primary institutions are dependent upon secondary institutions for their survival and development, but secondary institutions are informed by primary institutions for their purpose and meaning. If we lose this distinction, we tend to disorder the role business plays in human society.

## Family and Religion as Primary Institutions

For the Christian, family and church serve as the primary institutions of society. Family founded in marriage is the first vital cell of society in which economic and political institutions should be embedded. John Paul II tells us that the family is the place where we receive the first formative

[4] See Habiger Institute for Catholic Leadership, *True Leadership*, chaps. 13 and 14.

ideas about "what it means to love and to be loved, and thus what it actually means to be a person."[5] The family should be the place where we first experience goods shared in common.

Yet, the family needs something more than itself. The family by itself is prone to its own parochialism and tribalism and can insulate itself from the larger good of society. Like any ecosystem, institutions are dependent on other systems. Institutions need help from other institutions to flourish. When isolated, they tend to implode. The family, in particular, needs a transcendent source to connect it to the common good and to help it resist the tendency to self-absorption. That source is expressed through the institution of religion—in particular, the Church.

Mary Eberstadt captures this relationship when she speaks of the family and Church as the "double helix" that gives us our cultural DNA. The double helix is a biological discovery of two strands of DNA connected by units that make it look like a twisted rope ladder. This DNA helix gives us our physical make-up, from hair and eye color to our immune system. We inherit half from our mother and the other half from our father. Family and Church serve as the two strands of our cultural DNA. When connected to each other, the two strands reproduce and strengthen each

---

[5] John Paul II, Encyclical Letter on the Hundreth Anniversary of Rerum novarum *Centesimus annus* (May 1, 1991), §38.

other and give the society the cultural adhesive to flourish.[6]

The two primary institutions of family and Church nurture the foundational meaning that defines human culture. They help couples mature and develop. They foster the receptivity of children and their nurturing. They address our origins and birth, our destiny and death, and our vocation. They help us to know what to sacrifice, what to moderate, what to commit ourselves to. Simply put, they provide the fundamental root system to human culture.

## Business as a Secondary Institution

A business is a secondary institution because it cannot by itself adequately give primary meaning to peoples' lives. It cannot tell us of our origins or our destinies. Unfortunately, there are people who think it can. In an article in the *Harvard Business Review*, some thinkers argued that families and Churches have eroded as the cultural foundation of society and suggested that the "workplace is becoming a *primary* means for personal fulfillment.... More than providing work, companies can help give meaning to people's lives."[7] This way of thinking will never end well. We live in a time when secondary institutions, particu-

---

[6]  Mary Eberstadt, *How the West Really Lost God* (West Conshohoken, PA: Templeton Press, 2013), 22.

[7]  Christopher Bartlett and Sumantra Ghoshal, "Changing the Role of Top Management: Beyond Strategy to Purpose," *Harvard Business Review* (January–February 1995): 79–88, https://hbr.org/1995/01/changing-the-role-of-top-management-beyond-structure-to-processes.

larly business and the state, are more and more crowding out primary institutions by usurping their role and setting themselves up as alternative sources of meaning and identity. Secondary institutions such as business, necessary and useful as they are, need to honor their proper bounds. "First things first, second things second." Although it is certainly true that the family and Church have experienced a diminishing importance during the last fifty years, we cannot get more out of business than it is able to give.

## The Ordered Relationship between Primary and Secondary Institutions

When family and religion serve as the moral and spiritual DNA of culture, they do two very important things to orient business toward the common good. First, faith and family institutions limit economic activity so that there is natural space for people to foster right relationships with one another and with God. They resist the "total work mentality" expressed by writers in the *Harvard Business Review*. As Josef Pieper stated, we must "enlarge and widen our scope beyond work."[8]

Judaism accomplishes this enlarged scope partly through the practice of keeping the Sabbath, and Christianity, through the analogous keeping of the Lord's Day.[9]

---

[8]  See Josef Pieper, *Leisure*, chap. 4.
[9]  See John Paul II, Apostolic Letter on Keeping the Lord's Day Holy *Dies Domini* (May 31, 1998).

Abraham Joshua Heschel, the great twentieth century Jewish rabbi and theologian, sees the Sabbath as enabling a resistance to the encroaching claims of production and consumption, providing space and time for a human and religious identity beyond our roles as entrepreneurs, CEOs, consumers, citizens, and, for that matter, any identity claim that turns doing or having into being.[10]

Strong family life also limits economic activity by recognizing the covenantal bond between the couple and their care for children, a set of commitments requiring time and energy and often taking priority over the demands of work. In the family, our deepest identities as women and men begin to be formed as wives and husbands, sons and daughters, brothers and sisters, mothers and fathers. Short-circuiting these identities disorders our humanity. When a man founds his identity more on being an entrepreneur than on being a father, his life becomes disordered. As my fellow professor Robert Kennedy once said to me, "My children have only one father, my wife one husband. My students have more than one teacher."

Second, family and faith order economic activity and remind business of its purpose by connecting production and consumption to the common good and its participants to their particular vocations. When we see life in

---

[10] See Abraham Joshua Heschel, *The Sabbath: Its Meaning for Modern Man* (New York: Farrar, 2005).

ways that go beyond our work, we come back to our work with a deeper vocation to it. Fostering a contemplative outlook through prayer or through the Sabbath helps in developing a deep well of receptivity and gratitude that can shed light on the activities of the whole week.

The Lord's Day and the habits of silence, prayer, and worship help us to remember what we are prone to forget—namely, that we are created; that the earth is a gift with its own laws and demands; that human beings are a gift and not merely self-created; and that the world was created for all people, including the poor. Without this contemplative outlook, without moments of worship and adoration and sincere conversations with the Lord, Pope Francis laments that "our work easily becomes meaningless; we lose energy as a result of weariness and difficulties, and our fervor dies out."[11] Religious institutions with a mature social tradition help us to see that our work as a vocation calls us to give our talents and skills for the good of others.

The family also plays an important role in the meaning of work. As the first school of virtue, the family is the place where desires are matured, reason is formed, the will is shaped, and a community of persons is established. While businesses are not simply other families, they are to be *human* places of production. A family where the mother

---

[11] Francis, Apostolic Exhortation on the Proclamation of the Gospel in Today's World *Evangelii gaudium* (November 24, 2013), §262.

and father receive the gift of children and then give in building a family creates a pattern of receiving and giving that impacts the larger society, including business. Such a family instills in businesses a greater sense of responsibility and community as well as a readiness to protect and respect others even if such actions may not maximize profit.

These two functions of the family and Church, of *limitation* and *ordering*, help to properly embed business within the wider culture and impart to it the quality of a genuine human activity, rather than only an instrumental one.

Here we begin to touch on the important concept of the common good. We do not contribute to the common good by homogenizing differences to a "lowest common denominator," whether through government regulations or business "best practices." Rather, we contribute to the common good when we draw upon the particularity of the primary institutions of family and Church, which reveal to us who we are when we are at our best. It is only from the place of deep meaning that we connect the goods of business to what the Christian tradition calls the common good.

## II. BUSINESS THINKING: GETTING TO PURPOSE

Effective leaders articulate, cultivate, and execute the purpose of the institution they lead. Whether businesses, universities, families, or governments, every institution has a *raison d'etre*, a "reason for its being"—an account of why it exists and what it is "designed" to do. An institution's purpose clarifies (1) which goods are to be pursued by an institution and (2) how it orders such goods for the good of the whole. Good leaders define their institutional purpose as the common good—goods that are pursued and ordered in common. But the idea of the common good needs some elaboration.

The challenge with the common good is that it can be easily sloganized. We have to define what we mean by the phrase and how it can be used. According to Catholic social teaching, the standard description of the common good is "the sum total of *social conditions* which allow people, either as groups or as individuals, to reach their *fulfillment* more fully and more easily."[12] Let us focus for a moment on two elements of this description:

- *social conditions*—those things or goods that are usually necessary for people to attain their proper development of becoming persons in relation to others, and
- the actual attainment of *human fulfillment*, which includes the whole person and is shared by all members of the community.

These two elements of the common good can be likened to the action of a gardener who nurtures the soil through watering,

[12] Catechism of the Catholic Church, 1906 (emphasis added).

tilling, and fertilizing (social conditions), all of which increases the seeds' chance for growth (fulfillment). In a similar way, businesses should set up conditions for people to grow and help them to attain certain aspects of fulfillment. Let's take a closer look at both the social conditions created by business and what human fulfillment looks like there.

## Social Conditions of Business: Promoting Three Goods

One way to understand social conditions as related to specific institutions is to articulate the goods each institution generates for itself and the wider community. To begin to understand the goods of business, we might think about the specific goods of a person's work. Alasdair MacIntyre has noted three goods that make work meaningful:

- Good Work: "that the work that we do is and is recognized to be *our* work, *our* contribution, in which we are given and take responsibility for doing it and for doing it well";
- Good Goods: "that the work that we do has a point and purpose, is productive of genuine goods";
- Good Wealth: "that we are rewarded for doing [the work] in a way that enables us to achieve the goods of family and community."[13]

[13] Alasdair MacIntyre, "How Aristotelianism Can Become Revolution-

The three goods that characterize meaningful work have the same fundamental qualities that characterize meaningful business. This translates into three specific goods that a "good business" contributes to the social conditions of society:

- Good Work: business as an institution organizes work where employees develop their gifts and talents for themselves, but also for the business and for the larger community;
- Good Goods: business as an institution gives the world the products and services it needs, providing goods that are truly good and services that truly serve;
- Good Wealth: business as an institution creates sustainable wealth that distributes wealth justly to all stakeholders.

When businesses provide these three goods, they serve as the economic engine of a society and play an indispensable role in contributing to the common good. When they fail to achieve these goods, they frustrate the building up of the community. As we discussed at the beginning of the chapter, to say that business is simply about profit or

ary: Ethics, Resistance and Utopia," in *Virtue and Politics*, ed. Paul Blackledge and Kelvin Knight (Notre Dame, IN: University of Notre Dame Press, 2011), 323.

wealth cheapens the good that business can do.

We will explore each of these three goods in greater detail in the next three chapters. The point for now is that when businesses provide all three of these goods they contribute to the social conditions that tend to the proper development and flourishing of those in their environment. But this brings us to the most difficult part of our discussion. We will want to know: What does human flourishing—which the Church calls "integral human development"—look like in a business context?

## Fulfillment: Integral Human Development

Although the three goods of business are critically important for the common good, their achievement may not necessarily lead to the actual fulfillment of the persons involved in the business as a secondary institution. For example, William O'Brien, former CEO of Hanover Insurance Group, explained that even in workplaces where good products and services are generated, where good work is fostered through enlightened human resource practices, and where good wealth is created and distributed, people can still be disenchanted.[14] We can have all the goods in the world and still not be good. People can have great work, but still feel stagnated. Companies can have all the social conditions in place but still lack community and, ultimately, still lack integral human development. Why is this the case?

[14] William J. O'Brien, *Character at Work: Building Prosperity through the Practice of Virtue* (New York: Paulist Press, 2008), 104.

An allegory from Chinese literature on the surprising difference between hell and heaven can help us with this point.

> Hell is a room with a big table full of bowls of delicious steaming rice. People sit around the table, and each has chopsticks in his or her hands to eat the rice. However, the chopsticks are so long that nobody is able to eat, and instead pokes the others in the eyes and face. There ensues a constant and bitter fight, and consequently people starve in front of the bowls of food. Heaven is quite different. The room is the same, the table with the rice bowls is the same, even the chopsticks are just as long and cumbersome. However, instead of fighting, the diners feed each other in sublime harmony. They have a real common good.[15]

In hell, all the people have the goods—chopsticks, bowls, and rice, but their only interest is in feeding themselves. Hell is the fragmentation of individual preferences and interests. What makes heaven different from hell is not the "things." The difference is that people share together in the purpose of helping each other, developing the arts of cooperation and the bonds of communion and resulting

---

[15] Special thanks to Msgr. Martin Schlag, who shared this allegory with us.

in meaningful relationships.

There are two distinct ways that common goods are shared within community: sharing goods *with* diminishment and sharing goods *without* diminishment. For example, when an employee falls seriously ill, and other employees step in and share their sick leave, the number of sick days available is diminished, but solidarity among the employees is gained—both for the sick and the healthy.

Or, take a more ordinary business example. When an organization allocates a limited amount of resources, one group will get more and another less. When a business makes a profit off the prices they charge to the consumer, there is a limited amount they can distribute as bonuses, dividends, future wage increases, benefits, and investments. This distribution of wealth, however, is never a value-neutral activity. This is why the virtue of justice is important as it relates to the distribution of goods.

When, for example, a business fails to pay a living wage or when it gouges vulnerable customers on higher prices, the lack of justice prevents a proper community of persons to develop. But when this kind of sharing is done in justice, we arrive at what we call sharing without diminishment. When a business distributes its resources *justly,* justice is not allocated but participated in.

Here's how sharing without diminishment works: The second kind of sharing of goods happens without diminishment (participative goods). When a candle lights another candle, the first candle loses nothing of its light or quality. This fact is beautifully recreated at the Easter Vigil Mass when everyone's candle is lit from the Paschal candle and the church becomes full of light.

Similarly, when the purpose of a company is shared throughout the organization, nothing is diminished, but great power is generated throughout the company. "Shared purpose" is a critical success factor for world class companies, since it is one of those qualities of the firm that strengthens culture, morale, and engagement among all employees. "Doing one's own thing" is not energizing, at least not for long. We are created for more than just pursuing our own interests. We are meant to be working in relation with others—through institutions—to build the common good.

Let's return to the example above concerning wealth distribution: when a person is treated justly, he or she is more prone to respond with justice, and when two people are treating each other justly, they tend to trust each other more with decisions. They have less need for onerous contracts. They spend less time checking up on each other and are more willing to make sacrifices for the good of each other. They are more likely to stay at their company despite challenges and tensions, thus reducing turnover. All of these qualities contribute to the organizational culture and morale of the business. They make business more meaningful, usually more enjoyable, and in most cases, more effective.

In the Thomistic tradition, justice is defined as "right relationships," meaning the practice of giving to others what is due them. The virtue of justice is not diminished the more it is exercised. Rather, practicing justice strengthens the common bonds of those in the business. This is the way virtue works. Virtues begin to establish relationships that constitute genuine communities and are not merely contracts or transactions of mutually self-serving exchanges.

Relationships founded on virtue, especially justice, generate trust, loyalty, patience, and the ability to sacrifice, thus allowing people to do and accomplish more and better things with each other. They create synergistic effects that are real, if not easily measurable. Such bonds of communion are fostered through policies and structures that promote the good of the other, such as just wages, layoffs as a last alternative, fair prices, common ownership, and fair and reasonable payment schedules for suppliers. While such policies and practices do not guarantee bonds of communion, they bring a potent influence to bear on all those involved, leading to their integral human development.

In a business setting, these goods shared in common—these bonds of communion—are the threads of a strong cord that bind the various stakeholders in the company together: employee and employer, customer and producer, supplier and customer. Their presence or absence makes the difference between healthy or poor company morale, and they influence the level of trust (or mistrust) in a supplier relationship. When there is a proper sharing of goods, relationships that are not simply reducible to a metric of price or wage are fostered. Because such virtuous relationships are not easily measurable, they get little play in academic scholarship; many journals as well as businesses have made it a mantra that what can't be measured, can't be managed.

Nonetheless, the effects of such virtuous bonds of connection, involving what Peter Maurin, a founder of the Catholic Worker Movement, called "the art of human contacts," are not invisible. They can be encountered experientially in such things as the warmth of a greeting, the clear concern employers and employees have for one another, a handshake of agreement, a readiness to make time for conversation, a willingness to sacrifice for the common effort, and a generally low level of toxic gossip.

## CONCLUSION

Because we are created as social beings, institutions that carry on our various relationships through time and space are necessary and natural to us. It is therefore part of our vocation to be builders of institutions. Our primary institutions are family and Church. They are the primary sources of meaning for us, and they should inform all we do. Business is a secondary institution. Again, secondary does not mean unimportant. Without healthy and vibrant secondary institutions, primary institutions fray and weaken. This is why business must understand its purpose in terms of the common good.

The next three chapters will provide examples of business leaders who are confident in the good that business can do. We will examine in more concrete terms how businesses can promote the common good by exploring the practices and policies of good work, good goods, and good wealth.

CHAPTER 5

# GOOD WORK
## GIFT RECOGNITION AND COORDINATION

LIFE is a long and difficult walk, especially when we find ourselves in work that is boring, mechanical, bureaucratic, or repressive. The endurance act of waking up day after day can be depressing when we face an eight-, ten-, or twelve-hour day that grinds us away. This grind creates what Matthew Kelly calls "Q & S people"—those who quit but stay.[1] They disconnect from work, but they do enough to get the job done.

Life is, of course, an even longer and more difficult walk if we have no work at all. Yet, while work is toil, it does not need to be a grind. Work, like family and leisure, should develop us, not depress us.

Despite what Dilbert says, businesses have made a lot

---

[1] See Matthew Kelly, *The Four Signs of a Dynamic Catholic* (Cincinnati, OH: Beacon Publishing, 2012).

of progress in humanizing work. Programs and experiments such as work cells or pods, flat environments, self-managed or cross-functional teams, Total Quality Management, and quality circles, as well as strange-sounding programs such as holacracy, have been implemented to mitigate the mind-numbing characteristics of bureaucracy and to invite the gifts and talents of employees into their organizations.[2]

However, such programs are often killed by instrumentalizing managers who judge their use solely in terms of economic value. Kept from a deeper understanding of good work, employees eventually feel used and depersonalized. Instead of working to create conditions for the building of trust and loyalty within their organizations, managers can turn such programs into sloganish fads. It is no surprise that employees tend to respond to the latest fad with a great deal of cynicism.

What is needed in organizations today are sound principles that, on the one hand, recognize the essential economic reality of business, and on the other, insist that work is never merely an instrument to production, but a human activity with profound moral and spiritual meaning. One such leadership principle that can help with this is called *subsidiarity*.

[2]  Gary Hamel and Michele Zanini, "Excess Management Is Costing the U.S. $3 Trillion Per Year," *Harvard Business Review* (September 5, 2016), https://hbr.org/2016/09/excess-management-is-costing-the-us-3-trillion-per-year.

Subsidiarity is a word that doesn't roll easily off the tongue but is nonetheless worth understanding. At the heart of the principle of subsidiarity is the recognition that each working person has something to *give* to others. As leaders and workers, we need to *re-cognize* ("to know again") the diverse gifts, talents, abilities, and skills of all our employees. And having once recognized those gifts, we need to *coordinate* them for the good of the company and the society.

The ability to both recognize and coordinate the gifts of others sounds noble and enlightening, but it is not easy to practice. We all have blind spots. We often think that we respect and encourage others in their gifts far more than we actually do. As Mr. Darcy put the problem in Jane Austen's novel *Pride and Prejudice*, "I was given good principles, but left to follow them in pride and conceit."[3] My wife Teresa helped me to see how this pride and conceit was at work in my own life. It was, again in the words of Darcy, "a lesson, hard indeed at first, but most advantageous."[4]

My personal lesson went like this: In my naïve, self-righteous way, I mentioned to my wife one day my appreciation of the gifts of some of my colleagues at the University. What I thought was a nice and noble thought—but

[3] Jane Austen, *Pride and Prejudice* (London: J.M. Dent & Co., 1907), 319.
[4] Austen, *Pride and Prejudice*.

which was actually one of those moments of pride meant to let her know how virtuous I was—soon led us into a rather heated exchange. My wife called me out on my apparent "gift recognition," which was not as noble a sentiment as I had thought. She explained that I overvalued certain gifts, while seriously discounting others.

In the academy we value intelligence and high IQ, analytical skills, a sharp wit, the ability to "think critically," and the ability to debate with rhetorical flair. I have colleagues who are very smart and wise and who have taught me a tremendous amount over the years. But my wife saw something that I did not. My appreciation for these men (and yes, they were all men) clouded my vision and inhibited the recognition of the gifts of other men and women at the university.

I had discounted people who were less articulate but more intuitive, people whose intuitions were more in tune to reality and could see things as a whole, people whose IQ may not have been as high as certain colleagues, but whose EQ (emotional intelligences) was off the charts. These people were often less eloquent in stating their views, so their insights could be easily dismissed by myself and others. Yet they were more sensitive to other peoples' perspectives, caring about those on the margins and, in the process, often complicated decisions that needed to be made.

Teresa helped me acknowledge, not without a fair bit

of resistance from myself, that I was only seeing part of reality and not "seeing things whole." I was not acknowledging the full set of gifts in front of me, but was instead fixated on a part (those talents highly prized in the academy) and failing to see the multiple gifts needed to run an organization. I would be in rapt attention with some colleagues, all the while mechanically nodding my head to others and not really hearing them. While I thought I was good at gift recognition, I was seeing only *some* people's gifts while marginalizing others.

My failure in this case was a failure to practice subsidiarity. I needed to remember what I had forgotten and to see the gifts inherent in my various colleagues. Practicing subsidiarity helps us to recognize that the people in front us are not merely eight-hour units, cogs in the machine, or stakeholders with interests, but rather are immortal beings created in God's image. Their ability to exercise their gifts is key to their vocations and to their development as persons.

To help us remember these fundamental truths about ourselves and others, to bring subsidiarity to bear in our work environments, this chapter utilizes a simple age-old method called "see, judge, act." Thomas Aquinas called this method "practical wisdom," and Ignatius of Loyola called it "discernment."[5] In putting this trio into practice,

---

[5] See Thomas Aquinas, *Summa theologiae*, vol. 36: "Prudence" (2a2ae. 47-56), trans. Thomas Gilby (Cambridge: Cambridge University Press, 2006), q. 47, a. 8.

we will be able to *see* where subsidiarity is actually at work in our organization. We will be able to *judge* our situation from a stance with deep moral and spiritual roots. Finally, we will be able to *act* to bring about a deeper practice of subsidiarity in complex organizations. What follows is an exploration of some of the practices and metrics that can show how the principle of subsidiarity can foster good work in our organizations.

## SEEING THE SITUATION: ENGAGEMENT PROBLEMS

One indicator of good work is the active engagement of workers in their jobs. Studies reveal some problems here. In the US, a Gallup survey estimated that an average of two thirds of employees are either indifferent or hostile to their work. The survey put the price of employee disengagement costs at somewhere between 450–550 billion dollars annually.[6]

There are many reasons for disengagement in the workplace—low wages, poor upbringing and schooling, drugs and alcohol, and family problems—but one of the notable causes of lack of engagement has much to do with what we might call "bad work," and how leadership

---

[6] Gallup, *State of the American Workplace: Employee Engagement Insights for US Business Leaders* (Washington, DC, 2013): 5, 8–9, 12, http://www.gallup.com/strategicconsulting/163007/state-american-workplace.aspx.

designs work so poorly. Pope Pius XI explained this in 1931, writing that it is a scandal that "dead matter leaves the factory ennobled and transformed, while men are corrupted and degraded."[7] Think of an automobile factory. A whole assortment of materials comes into the factory and comes out as a brand new car. It is an extraordinary feat of human ingenuity to make such a product. But why is it that when *people* go into such a factory, they sometimes come out dulled and numbed?

Business people, as well as all people, need to recognize the difference between the subjective and objective dimensions of work, a distinction made by John Paul II. Business leaders are often practiced in developing a whole series of metrics, scorecards, and incentives to measure and achieve the goals of the objective dimensions of work, such as output related to quality, plant efficiency, profits, and inventory turns. Such metrics tell us something about how well we are doing in creating goods and services and how much wealth are we creating (good goods and good wealth). We are hired, evaluated, rewarded, and fired based on how we perform according to the standards of the objective dimension of work.

But when it comes to the subjective dimension of work—those changes that take place within us—we can be

---

[7] Pius XI, Encyclical Letter on Reconstruction of the Social Order *Quadragesimo anno* (May 5, 1931), §135.

blind to what our work does to us. However impressive the objective accomplishments of our work in communications, computerization, construction, or travel, our work does not stop there. As workers, we not only change the world but we also change ourselves. Yet, as the Russian novelist Leo Tolstoy reminds us, "everyone thinks of changing the world, but no one thinks of changing himself."[8]

When a manager, a teacher, a technician, a lawyer, or a plumber works, he or she affects the inner landscape of his or her character. It is not a question here of whether we change, but how we change, and this brings us to moral and spiritual matters. Practicing subsidiarity helps us to get to the deeper roots of this moral and spiritual reality. At a minimum this practice will mean that there is work to be done, that it is safe, that the work conditions are not debilitating, that employees are spoken to and treated respectfully, and that there is no tolerance of harassment or of a hostile work environment. Such practices are a kind of low bar for the workplace. The highly principled leader will want to go beyond this minimum. To gain a fuller understanding of good work, we need to delve yet more deeply into the meaning of subsidiarity.

---

[8] Leo Tolstoy, quoted in Mark A. Bryan, Julia Cameron, and Catherine A. Allen, *The Artist's Way at Work: Riding the Dragon* (New York: William Morrow, 1999), 160.

## JUDGING: SUBSIDIARITY AND THE LOGIC
## OF GIFT

In the introduction to this book, I noted that one of the temptations for business leaders as well as for all of us is that we have adopted principles that exist like cut flowers: they look pretty and smell nice, but because they have no roots, they are fads with a quick shelf life. When business leaders view subsidiarity as a productivity technique—not a moral principle but an instrumental one—programs such as cross-functional work teams, holacracy, or quality circles tend to collapse under the weight of an instrumental rationality.

When Pius XI introduced subsidiarity into the Catholic social teaching lexicon in 1931, his fundamental concern was that the state was absorbing too much of life such that the unique gifts of family, education, voluntary associations, and the Church—often known as "civil society"—were being suppressed. The same process of absorption can be seen in the business world, where the corporation comes to exercise a similar suppression of gifts.

Sixty years after Pius XI wrote about subsidiarity, Bill Pollard, CEO of Service Master, said something similar: "We must as leaders embrace the principle of subsidiarity. It is wrong to steal a person's right or ability to make a decision."[9] When we design work that fails to take into consideration employees' gifts and talents, this work actually kills the human spirit; decisions are stolen, responsibilities are absorbed, and gifts are designed out of the work.

The roots of subsidiarity are found in a deeper logic than a merely instrumental one. It is grounded in the logic of gift. Benedict XVI describes subsidiarity as respecting "personal dignity by recognizing in the person a subject who is always capable of *giving* something to others."[10] At the heart of subsidiarity is gift recognition. When we encounter an employee, do we just see an 8-hour unit, a function of functionality, a utility enhancer, a producer of goods, something useful? We should see these things, actually. Employees must be useful. If they are not, they must either be helped through training and development or the manager needs to let them go. Unproductive employees drag a business down into bankruptcy.

But do we also see the invisible reality, the dignity of the person, the image of God, his or her relationships and friendship? Do we see the inherent gifts of our fellow employees? The danger is that we get fixated on the economic and physical and fail to see the spiritual—all that the person has to give. God has endowed each of us with what

---

[9] William Pollard, *The Soul of the Firm* (Downers Grove, IL: Harper Business, 1996), 102.

[10] Benedict XVI, Encyclical Letter on Integral Human Development in Charity and Truth *Caritas in veritate* (June 29, 2009), §57.

the Christian tradition calls *munera*—gifts. God is not a micromanager; He calls us to exercise our gifts, which is precisely the way by which we grow as human beings.

Subsidiarity reveals that to create conditions in which employees' gifts can be exercised is rooted in God's creative act, in the way we were made. We develop as persons when we exercise our gifts. Made in God's image, we are meant to work in participation with the action of the Creator. Creation itself is our model for subsidiarity. It is a revealed truth about creation that "God has not willed to reserve to himself all exercise of power."[11] Instead, God has entrusted certain gifts and roles to each creature. The exercise of these gifts contributes to living out a vocation. Exercising our capacity for self-gift—sharing our gifts, talents, abilities, and skills with others—is one of the fundamental ways we manifest the *imago Dei*.

Gifts endow us with the capacity to act for more than ourselves. They are meant to be given away, not hoarded. Our gifts do not belong to us but they are to go through us to others.[12] And when they serve others, that service reflects back upon us in terms of our own development as persons (the subjective dimension of work). If we behave as though our gifts are only for us, we rob others, dishonor God's created order, and corrupt ourselves.

[11] Cf. Catechism of the Catholic Church, 307, 302.
[12] See Habiger Institute, *True Leadership*.

## ACTING: OPERATIONALIZING SUBSIDIARITY

So how does subsidiarity work at work? How do we recognize our own gifts, talents, strengths, and skills and those of others, and how do we coordinate them within the structure of a business that needs to produce good goods and achieve good wealth? Leaders who can simultaneously manage the two perspectives of recognition and coordination are powerful agents of transformation.

First, let's look a bit more at gift recognition. Everyone is gifted in various and unique ways. We do not come out of the womb with a clean slate. Each of us has different inherent gifts that have the potential to become distinct strengths and skills. Some are born with higher levels of IQ, EQ, physical coordination, intuition, empathy, or organization abilities. If these gifts are not exercised by learning and acquiring skills through knowledge and discipline, they either lie dormant or get exercised with eventual frustration and disorder. I often meet with students, acquaintances, or friends who are wrestling at different stages of life with a similar set of questions: "What am I called to do?" "What are my gifts?" "Am I using them in the right place?" These are not easy questions to answer, but certain basic truths can be a helpful starting point.

As the director of the Center for Catholic Studies, I oversee our Leadership Internship Program for undergraduates. One element of the program is helping stu-

dents discern their gifts, talents, and skills and how and
where they can bring them to their work. One way to
get at discerning gifts is by attending to what we desire.
We naturally desire to exercise what we are gifted to do.
While our desires can be uninformed and disordered, they
do tell us something. Such desires need testing, but they
are important clues. Because our gifts have been given to
us, as part of the created order they naturally bring us energy, passion, and purpose. We can begin our assessment
by asking questions such as: Why is it that I find energy
and excitement in making things, in history, in numbers,
in organizing, in teaching? Can I make a living from this?
Where do I think I can make a difference? Where do I
find myself inspired to try?

Recognizing gifts in ourselves and in others is not
always easy. We find ourselves in a fallen world, and we
ourselves are fallen, so for a wide variety of reasons, we
can drift and wander from our gifts. We can disorder our
talents. The more a gift is separated from its divinely in-
tended meaning and application, the more we will find
ourselves lost and at sea, gradually falling into greater
angst and boredom. We also need to be clear of those
habits and addictions that dull our minds and hearts such
as alcohol, drugs, pornography, mindless entertainment,
and the ubiquity of screen time. What we need is silence,
prayer, adoration, Scripture, and sacraments, all of which

help us to see an enlarged world of creation. We also need counsel from those who see in us gifts that we can't see—trusted counselors who can "cure us of our illusions, and encourage us in our timidities."[13]

While gift recognition is important, gifts also need to be coordinated in a business such that it can produce a product or service and do so at a profit. Informed by subsidiarity, businesses can coordinate the gifts of their workers by doing three things: (1) designing work well, (2) educating and equipping employees, and (3) trusting that those employees will do their work well.

As to designing work well: the trick is to design work such that it taps the gifts, talents, and skills of employees, while at the same time keeping the organization competitive in the marketplace by improving efficiency, quality, and profitability. These two qualities are not always easy to get right.

Howard Rosenbrock, a manufacturing engineer, has pointed out that engineers often design work that requires only a fraction of a person's talents, skills, and knowledge. If they were to "consider people as though they were robots," he wryly commented, they would "provide them with less trivial and more human work."[14] Most engineers

---

[13] Habiger Institute, *True Leadership*, 94.

[14] Howard H. Rosenbrock, "Engineers and the Work That People Do," in *The Experience of Work*, ed. Craig R. Littler, (Aldershot, UK: Gower in association with The Open University, 1985), 161–171, http://ieeecss.org/CSM/library/1981/sept/w04-8.pdf.

would not design a machine and use only ten percent of its capacity, but they too often design jobs that only use a fraction of human talent. Such mechanistic and technocratic attitudes can prevent them from seeing the gifts, abilities, and talents of their employees. On the other hand, if work is designed humanely but fails to compete in the industry, the result is not good work but bankruptcy.

The second coordinating task for leaders is to teach and equip employees. While it is true that when people bring their skills and knowledge into an organization, they add to its "collective intelligence," this collective intelligence does not just happen of its own accord. To make subsidiarity work, leaders need to assist (*subsidium*) and strengthen their people through effective education, training, mentoring, counsel, and evaluation, so that their gifts are effectively coordinated within the company's overall project. Defining employees' work broadly while neglecting to aid them through education and equipment is a recipe for failure, both for the employee and for the organization.

The third task is to establish strong relationships with employees, beginning with delegation and moving to trust. When business leaders accept responsibility for developing employees, delegation becomes a mini-classroom for both leaders and employees. They test performance with increasing levels of risk and trust: from carrying out orders, to independent choices where the costs of failure are low, to consultation and feedback (early stages), to full participation with leaders in decision making (advanced stages), and finally to independent problem solving (full trust).

One example that exhibits these three elements of recognition and coordination coming together is the experience of Reell Precision Manufacturing as they redesigned their assembly line from a "Command-Direct-Control" style of management, in which managers made all the decisions concerning the assembly area, to a "Teach-Equip-Trust" style of management, in which employees were taught inspection procedures, equipped with quality instruments, and trusted to do things right on their own assembly-lines.

The company did not come to this change by a deductive moral argument, but rather because they faced a practical problem that needed to be solved. A particular product line called for an independent evaluation of samples by Quality Control after each setup was complete and before the job was run. The problem they faced was in dealing with the necessary time required for the setup to be approved by the quality controller. The setup person would submit samples to Quality Control, but usually have to wait several hours until the inspector was available to evaluate. By that time, the setup person had usually gone on to the next job. This meant that if the samples were not satisfactory, it would take even more time before adjustments could be made. In some cases, the process needed to be repeated several times before the job was approved. Manufacturing found this frustrating because they would find themselves setting up jobs and not being able to run them for several days.

Someone asked the question, "What if we taught the setup people to do their own inspection and trusted them to do it right?" While the person who asked this question had probably never heard of the principle of subsidiarity, he or she was putting the principle into practice by recognizing and coordinating the gifts of the employees on the line. After restructuring the work process such that it tapped the skills and talents of the assembly workers, many benefits ensued. The employees decreased setup times for new products, reduced the need for quality inspection, increased overall quality, and required less supervision. By reducing these costs, the company not only created more humane work but also became more profitable and was able to increase its wage rates.[15]

What is interesting about this case is its inductive character. It started with a problem that needed to be solved and led to the redesigning of work, demanding greater education and equipping of employees, and a deeper trust in the workers. Yet, while it started off as a practical problem, it ended with a new philosophy of work

[15] See Michael Naughton and David Specht, *Leading Wisely in Difficult Times: Three Cases of Faith and Business* (New York: Paulist Press, 2011).

that Reell calls Teach-Equip-Trust. This led to greater productivity, better quality products, the growth of coworkers, and a better overall company culture.

This mini case gives us some key insights about subsidiarity:

1. Subsidiarity reduces bureaucracy by driving decision-making to the appropriate level of the organization. At Reell, instead of keeping the decision at the engineering level with quality control, decisions were located at the place where the work was done. Coworkers were entrusted with decision-making and responsibility according to their gifts and skills.

2. Subsidiarity reduces the amount of time managers must check their employees' decisions. Previously, the assembly process at Reell required five weeks for making, inspecting, and stocking sub- and final assemblies. After the redesign, all sub-assemblies and inspections were done in one continuous flow process by production workers. The entire process took less than two minutes and the finished unit was ready for shipment without further inspection when it came off the assembly line.

3. Subsidiarity leads to greater trust in the company. Reell's Direction Statement explains that

"instead of driving each other toward excellence, we strive to free each other to grow and express the excellence that is within all of us." The Teach, Equip, Trust model entails a confidence that coworkers will bring their full gifts and skills to the work of the company.

At Reell, this new philosophy of work contributed to some impressive metrics:

- Higher employee and customer engagement/satisfaction scores (net promoter scores)
- More robust education/training budgets for developing job skills
- Numerous internal promotions
- Lower turnover
- Higher level of safety
- Less absenteeism
- Fewer quality defects

When business leaders are well grounded in the moral and spiritual roots of subsidiarity, they tend to take on certain characteristics. For one, they expect their employees to work independently and to take prudent risks in what they do. The prudence is framed around the shared vision of the company. For another, they admit their own failures and model what it means to learn and grow from one's mistakes. A third characteristic is their good knowledge of their employees. They are not distant from their employees; they know them and their work. They often work beside them on certain projects and they take an interest in what they are doing. They spend time observing, coaching, counseling, and evaluating their employees, getting to know their strengths and weaknesses. They know the families of their coworkers, the sports their children are involved in, the challenges they are having. They talk with them meaningfully and with respect. They are aware of how much progress their people have made and what responsibilities they are ready to shoulder, and they have taken the time to craft customized development plans for them.

## CONCLUSION

The insights of this chapter on the principle of subsidiarity have come through several practitioners I have met along the way. Pierre Lecocq was the first CEO I encountered who spoke about "subsidiary leadership." I was soon to find out that Bill Pollard had been implementing that kind of leadership at Service Master for years. Bob Wahlstedt and Kyle Smith from Reell did not use the term "subsidiarity" at first, but they embodied it as leaders.

The witness of these leaders can help us to avoid the highly instrumental rationality that has moved businesses to view their workers in terms of the titles such as "human resources," and "human capital." When workers and their work are seen only as extensions of capital structures of profitability, subsidiarity can be seen as yet one more productivity technique, an attitude that fails to get to the deeper values that the sharing of gifts can provide.

More recently, I met Yves de Talhouët, Chairman of Faiencerie de Gien, at a conference on business and subsidiarity in Brazil. He has captured well the increasing problem of "proceduralism" in leadership, a tendency that creates a significant obstacle for subsidiarity leadership. He located the problem in larger organizations where sophisticated management systems have been developed to help monitor and capture the various activities of the company. Such systems are constructed with powerful software, analytics tools, and so on. Activities are divided into thin slices and observed from every possible angle. These systems create aggregates, ratios, indicators, and KPIs (key performing indicators), and generate KPI score cards. Benchmarks are then established to compare the organization with the rest of the industry, and best practices are established to achieve high scores.

Talhouët laments the fact that middle management must spend much of its time feeding these management systems with information necessary to produce the numbers. It means that they spend less time developing their people. Real work and real workers become invisible. As organizations get larger and more sophisticated, they can become fixated on the procedures, processes, structures, and rules necessary to carry the organization. Business leaders can tend to default to such systems for answers to all their issues and problems. These bureaucratic default settings become more and more selective about what information gets considered and more and more narrow about what they measure. Managers become more and more connected to the system and less and less connected to people.

While this development is certainly concerning, Talhouët concludes that when overly bureaucratic and technocratic procedural methods start to take on a life of their own, they force business leaders to recognize the problem of "bad work" and the need to address the situation with deeper principles. This, at least, is a good sign.

CHAPTER 6

# Good Goods
## Goods That Are Truly Good

I teach in a department called Catholic Studies where we foster an interdisciplinary vision that sees things in relation to each other to help students form judgments about the overall nature of realities they encounter. In one of the courses on faith and business, I team-teach with a colleague from the business school. When we discuss good goods—the products and services that a business creates—and markets, we ask our students three questions. First, "Are there bad goods in business?" If products are legal and profitable but of dubious social value, such as violent video games, pornography, adultery dating sites, cigarettes, high octane alcohol, abortifacients, gambling, usury (rent-to-own services with exorbitant interest rates), certain kinds of weapons, cheat sheet websites, so-called "gentleman clubs," and so forth, can we call them bad?[1]

For those students who have caught the relativistic, financially-concerned bug, the only bad goods are those that are illegal and that do not maximize profit. Business is simply a means to an end, and that end is profit. In their minds, if health care maximizes profit, that's great, but if marketing tobacco does the job just as well, so be it.

Other students are less crass, but their underlying logic is not much better. Rather than making shareholders king of business, they make customers king; the customer comes first and is always right. The choices of the customer are definitive and must reign. If people are freely willing to pay for something, they should be able to do so. Along with this view comes the idea that consumers—not producers—are responsible for whatever they use. If a product causes cancer, and the customer is informed about it and consents to pay the price for it, then it is the customer who has to live with the consequences. Consent alone—not what is being consented to—determines moral validity for the producer.

Our class discussions are usually lively on this topic, but they remain abstract until we go on to the second question: "Would you work for a company that produced cigarettes, weapons, pornography, or violent video games?"

---

[1] My colleague John McVea developed a series of mini cases on "bad goods," which serves as the basis of our class discussions.

With this question, things get more concrete and personal. For some students, the answer is no, but as good relativists, they often respond with a line like, "If someone wants to work for such a company, that is his choice. Who am I to judge?" For others, the answer depends entirely on the salary available, alternative job offers, and other matters of practical detail. They have their price and are ready to name it.

It is the third question that causes the most hesitation: "Are these goods worthy of you? Are they worth your time and life? And what does a life look like when you produce such goods over a lifetime?" Here we touch on the concept of good work and the subjective dimension of work examined in the last chapter. Such questions are important because they help our students to move from the abstract principles of the market and the law to more personal matters of conviction, character, virtue, vocation, giftedness, and witness—especially the witness they give to their future children, spouse, parents, and the larger community.

This line of questioning is not entirely new to our students. Many of them want meaning and relevance in their working lives. They want to create and produce goods that make a difference in the world. They are not just about the money. A number of them are attracted to "social entrepreneurship," where they can contribute to "goods that are truly good and services that truly serve."[2] They enjoy stories of entrepreneurs and companies who have created products and services that serve the society through microfinance, social investment, fair trade products, renewable energy, life-saving medical devices, and affordable housing, or people who work for vulnerable populations such as those in crisis pregnancies or those just out of prison. They find such examples inspiring and life-giving. They want to be a part of endeavors that improve human living. As a teacher, I can feel pretty good about myself when my students start to connect good goods with the larger principle of the common good. I think we are making progress—until I come to the uneasy feeling that we have just banished most of what happens in business to the margins.

Here is the problem. While these students avoid the abstractions of the market and the law, they can become overly romantic about what comprises a good. They reduce good goods to a narrow set of products and services provided by so-called "social businesses." While we and our students may avoid the crass ditch of consumerism and profit

[2] Dicastery for Promoting Integral Human Development, *Vocation of the Business Leader: A Reflection* (Vatican City: Vatican Press, 2014), https://www.stthomas.edu/media/catholicstudies/center/ryan/publications/publicationpdfs/vocationofthebusinessleaderpdf/FinalTextTheVocationoftheBusinessLeader.pdf, §40. See also Kenneth Goodpaster, "Goods That Are Truly Good, and Services That Truly Serve," *Journal of Business Ethics* 100, supp. 1 (January, 2012): 9–16.

maximization, we can fall into the opposite ditch (for every road has two ditches) of an unrealistic romanticism.

A conversation I had years ago with one of the finest businesspersons I know, Bob Wahlstedt, can help illustrate the problem. Bob, one of the three founders of Reell, told me that despite his company's success, he wished he could have built something that had saved lives, such as cardio pacemakers, instead of clutches for copiers and hinges for laptop computers. Bob had always seen good work for his co-workers as a key company virtue, but he was less impressed with the specific goods his company had brought out. To be sure, as an engineer, he had delighted in creating well-engineered products. He had kept a listening ear to his customers and their needs, enabling him and his colleagues to design products that were of superior quality and that were delivered on time. But at the end of the day they were still just hinges and clutches.

Bob was grappling with the question we were asking our students: Is this product or service worthy of you? I asked Bob this question: What if everyone made cardio pacemakers or medical devices? What if the only kind of businesses people would invest their energy in were those that visibly improved our society? Obviously, we'd be in trouble. The infrastructure necessary for a functioning society, one that promotes human development, entails a multitude of products and services, including hinges and clutches, bolts, mortgages, software, toilets, waste removal, plastic, roads, boots, clothes, and food products, along with pacemakers, microcredit, imaging medical devices, fair trade practices, and other such goods and services. It does not help us to be overly romantic about how we define good goods. A good society needs many different kinds of products and services to run, and the common good entails much more than just life-saving medical devices.

But we still face some tough questions when it comes to good goods. To make the question even stranger and more linguistically awkward, we could ask: What makes a good good *good*? If law and profit are not enough to define a good good, are there distinctions about the nature of various products and services that can help us to an answer? And more importantly, is there a connection between what we make and who we are?

Our desire to make things, like all of our desires, is God-given, but prone to disorder. Which principles should guide our desire to create goods that are truly good and services that truly serve? What disorders do we need to watch out for? As we will discuss below, when products or services are injurious to us, it is not usually by their nature—though examples such as pornography clearly are—but by their use—whether too much, misdirected, or disordered. As our society becomes increasingly morally diverse and pluralistic, business leaders find themselves in more situations where they need to think deeply about whether the goods they produce are truly good and the services they provide truly serve. We will explore three principles originating in the Christian tradition that aid us in clarifying the topic of good goods: (1) the universal destination of goods, (2) the relationship between needs and wants, and (3) the classic moral distinction between material and formal cooperation.

## I. THE UNIVERSAL DESTINATION OF GOODS AND THE CHALLENGE OF NEGATIVE EXTERNALITIES

To answer our grammatically challenged but important question "What makes a good good *good?*" a helpful place to start is with what some have called the *nobility of the mundane.* The popular Christmas movie *It's a Wonderful Life* brings out this quality in a powerful way. The banker, George Bailey, played by Jimmy Stewart, is unable to see the good he is doing in the mortgages he provides in the small town of Bedford Falls. In despair, he wishes he had never been born, and his wish is granted. He is then allowed to enter Bedford Falls as if he never lived, and it is here that he begins to see the importance of his life. This is a common problem for us. While it is important for us to see the moral gaps where our aspirations and our execution are not aligned, we also, like George Bailey, fail to see the moral bridges of the good we are doing.

Most of the products and services to which we have access are good goods made and delivered by businesses: credit, hinges, food, shelter, clothing, communications, insurance, transportation, medicine, and so forth. Through a great deal of innovation, creativity, and initiative, businesses and entrepreneurs invent and improve new ways of meeting consumers' needs. This relationship between producer and consumer involves multiple dimensions—design, functionality, price, quality, and service. Businesses coordinate people's gifts, talents, energies, and skills to serve the needs of customers. They anticipate needs, innovate, and build trust, often going beyond what their customers are looking for. It is all done so well and so often that we tend to take it for granted.

Take, for example, the food industry. Businesses like Cargill, Bimbo, Kraft, Aldi, and thousands of small- to medium-sized companies, cooperatives, and farms, have designed efficient methods of production and distribution to significantly bring down the cost of food, allowing families—especially the poor—to spend a smaller percentage of their income on food.

Most of us take this for granted. We expect to be able to find any food product that we want—fresh and safe— all year round at a low price. Behind this availability is a lot of hard work. In talking to those who do the harvesting, production, logistics, and packaging of food, one sees the hard work and complex systems needed to make this happen. We need to recognize the good that is being done. The food that businesses help produce brings about the universal destination of goods by making the goods of the earth accessible at prices that a large number of people can access. Without business, this principle would be poorly executed.

That is the moral good of business, but there are moral gaps as well. As great as the benefits of the food industry have been, there are problems within it. Agricultural businesses have at times been criticised for not covering the full cost of their products. For example, practices that bring higher yields can cause soil erosion. But the full costs of environmental degradation resulting from such by-products of production are not borne by producers and current customers but instead shifted onto the wider public, future generations, and often the poor. Economists call these costs "negative externalities," which have the effect of socializing the costs of production but privatizing the profits. Goods cannot be truly good when they violate the good of the natural environment, and in particular, when they place unreasonable burdens on the least culpable and most affected.

The production of good goods must include ways to address the negative externalities of waste. While this problem of developing an ecological production system is not easy to solve, some companies are providing life cycle assessments of their products and services and are reducing their waste, finding ways to recycle, and decarbonizing their energy use.

For example, the company Timberland creates shoes, boots, and other apparel. These products are good goods in that they provide footwear for the world. But Timberland has also taken responsibility for the effects of what they produce. They have significantly reduced chemicals linked to human or environmental harm by moving to water-based adhesives that reduce solvent use. They have designed their boots and shoes as a recyclable product by selecting raw materials that can be reused more easily. They have also sought to decarbonize their buildings and factories by implementing renewable energy sources and more energy-efficient cooling and heating systems, thus reducing energy consumption and carbon dioxide emissions.[3]

Developing new pollution-reducing technologies and using renewable sources of energy help to promote sustainable development. Organizations such as Timberland and hundreds of others are finding creative and innovative ways to harmonize production with an environmental mode of operation. Yet in the final analysis we cannot completely rely upon a market cycle or a technological fix

---

[3]  See J. Austin, H. Leonard, and J. Quinn, *Timberland: Commerce and Justice* (Boston, MA: Harvard Business School Publishing, 2004).

to solve the environmental problems we face. Ultimately, the cause of the problem is not only technical but also moral and spiritual.

Pope Francis has emphasized this point by calling for a lifestyle change that confronts a particularly modern view of a global consumerism, a view that is increasing in cultural dominance and homogeneity. He warns that a consumerism fixated on pleasures tends to blunt the conscience and leave no room for others—especially children, the poor, and God.[4] Our throwaways may be recyclable, but if we have become spiritually impoverished, we cannot flourish. We can only survive. This is why we have to be clear about the second of our principles: the distinction between *needs* and *wants*.

## II. THE DISTINCTION BETWEEN NEEDS AND WANTS AND THE PROBLEM OF CONSUMERISM

Too often when we think of "needs" we think of those basic goods essential for survival. This is not helpful. These are certainly needs, but surviving is not what the Church means when she speaks of integral human development. Instead of thinking of needs as essential for survival, think of them as basic conditions necessary to flourish as human beings. For example, do I need games in my house?

---

[4] See Francis, *Evangelii gaudium*, §2.

To survive, I do not, but to thrive, I do. Families, and particularly children, need to play games at home to help build joyful relationships.

When we speak of needs, we are talking about those conditions that help us to develop into who we are created to be. This is key to the common good that was discussed in chapter four. My colleague Robert Kennedy explains that although we need oxygen, food, shelter, and so on, we are not mere animals. As intelligent, free, and social creatures we also need and yearn for "knowledge, opportunities to exercise our creativity, interaction with other persons (there is a reason that Facebook is so hugely successful), but also beauty, recreation, and even challenges."[5]

Our "wants," on the other hand, are not necessary for our flourishing. They can be harmless, but they are always on the verge of either moving into immoderation and exploitation or being ordered to needs and utility. If I fail to moderate my intake of candy bars, I fall into unhealthy habits. But my want for the candy bar can also move to a need by its use. I can buy the candy bar to share with my son or daughter for a special treat, which bonds us together.

Our needs, then, are related to those things that we call "genuine goods," which help us to flourish. Wants, on the other hand, are those things that are either neutral or detrimental to our flourishing. Even if neutral at first, however,

---

[5] Robert Kennedy, unpublished notes.

our wants are never neutral for long. They either point to our desire to flourish, or they impel us into buying trivial, futile, or harmful goods, which can lead to consumerism.

So, do the products and services we produce meet consumer needs, or do they pander to consumers' wants? Although good goods give real value to consumers and serve the needs of the larger community, we also have to confront the problem of consumerism, which orients people to be more concerned about what they have and less concerned about who they become in having.[6]

We see the ugliness of consumerism in those companies that pander to wants through the sale of non-therapeutic drugs, cigarettes, pornography, gambling, violent video games, frivolous entertainment, and other such products. These products appeal to pleasure, fame, and wealth by exploiting people's base desires, insecurities, and fantasies. Such products have addictive qualities and have done largely untold damage not only to individuals but to marriages and families and the broader culture. While the existence of companies that provide such products and services is a serious problem in our society, we need to first confront the more foundational problem of consumerism. It has to do with how we understand freedom. The problem of consumerism may be more ubiquitous than we think.

One of the underlying values of our market-based

---

[6]  John Paul II, *Centesimus annus*, §36.

system is freedom. But how we understand that freedom, especially in terms of our choices among products and services, determines whether we flourish or become enslaved, whether we serve the good with excellence or grow indifferent to it. Having a choice between one hundred different cereal brands does not make us free, especially if our choice leads to obesity. What makes us free is the ordering of our choices to health. Our freedom always involves more than whether we choose this or that; it touches on the good judgments of the choice itself. This is why the distinction between wants and needs is so important.

The Ten Commandments, for example, are negative prohibitions—but not because God is a nasty ruler intent on keeping people from having fun. Rather, our "nos" in life clarify the "yeses" of our commitments. The alcoholic's no to a drink is a yes to relationships and development. The husband's no to pornography is a yes to fidelity to his wife. Our wants for food, drink, and sex are ordered by our need for relationship and fidelity. Without the riverbanks there is no direction for the river, and soon there is no river; it simply dissipates. Commandments, moral convictions, and virtues that impose limits are not threats to our integral human development; they are necessary boundaries for a meaningful life and meaningful business. They prevent our lives from dissipating into an array of choices that leave us committed only to our own desires.

Ashley Madison, an adultery dating site that uses the motto "Life is short. Have an affair," gives its fifty million members the choice to cheat on their spouses. This choice, however, does not give freedom to its consumers, but rather helps destroy their relationships, families, communities, and the common good—for a disordered desire and a fleeting moment of pleasure. It is the truth—not our choice—that sets us free. Our choices either cooperate with this truth or violate it.

We can more clearly understand these insights into freedom through an important distinction between the freedom *of* indifference and the freedom *for* excellence.[7] Simply put, our freedom of indifference is a so-called freedom that pays no attention to our needs, a common human nature, a common good, or God. It is a freedom from religion, parents, institutions, and any notion of truth, such that individuals can choose what they want. When exercising freedom of indifference, the highest value is the choice itself and not the content of the choice. This is the kind of freedom at the heart of consumerism. What matters is simply that one chooses, and the more choices available, the better.

Freedom for excellence, however, is based on the idea that we are made *for* something—that we *need* certain

---

[7]   See Servais Pinckaers, *Sources of Christian Ethics* (Washington, DC: Catholic University of America Press, 1995), 354–378.

things for our true fulfillment. It is the freedom to commit to authentic and binding relationships that provides the context for developing our internal capacities as human beings. All of this points to the virtues. Virtues are habits of excellence that bring out the best in us. Freedom for excellence is not merely concerned about the number of choices we have, but, more importantly, about the nature of the choices we make. This notion of excellence is necessary to understand freedom because "our choices are the prime indicators of our destiny."[8] Our choices form us into a particular kind of person. They are not discrete, arbitrary acts without consequences; they tend to the molding of character. "We actually become eternally what we have given ourselves to."[9]

What bearing does this distinction between the freedom of indifference and the freedom for excellence mean for our discussion of good goods? Steven Goldstone, CEO of the former company RJR Nabisco (a producer of tobacco as well as food products), argued in an interview that the production of cigarettes was a good good because it increased people's choices.[10] Goldstone was articulating the freedom of indifference. He saw his job as offer-

[8]  John F. Kavanaugh, "Last Words," *America: The Jesuit Review*, January 2002, 23.

[9]  Kavanaugh, "Last Words," 23.

[10]  Steven Goldstone, interview by Jim Lehrer, *The News Hour with Jim Lehrer*, PBS, January 29, 1998, video, https://archive.org/details/tobacco_ovy27a00. Accessed August 2, 2018.

ing people choices, not determining what those choices should be (although his company was spending a lot of advertising dollars to do just that).

Goldstone's view of freedom leads him to believe that he stands on neutral moral ground; that he has no responsibility to provide non-harmful goods or services, only to provide whatever people may be willing to pay for. He and many in business who think like him feel absolved of any responsibility for the effects of their goods and services on others. But this is a very dangerous disposition. This failure to distinguish between good and bad products and services not only unhooks businesspeople from any responsibility for the effects their products and services may have on consumers, but it also evaporates the meaning of their own actions.

Consumerism is a serious cultural and spiritual poverty plaguing the West. Under its influence, our identities are reduced to those of consumers, and we lose our true identities as Christians, mothers, fathers, citizens, and students. We are left with nothing but our arbitrary choices, often unaware of the malformation they are bringing about in us and our children.

## III. MATERIAL AND FORMAL COOPERATION: DISCERNING THE AMBIGUOUS

Of course, most of us do not work in tobacco, pornography, or violent entertainment companies, but this should not keep us from asking the challenging question: "Are we cooperating with forms of cultural pollution? And if we are, do we even know it?" This question came to me from a thoughtful group of faithful employees from the Target Corporation in Minneapolis. Let me give some background.

An interesting development in corporate America is the rise of interest groups within companies, such as women, gays, evangelicals, transgendered people, African Americans, and Hispanics. Such groups meet on a regular basis to talk about the challenges and opportunities in corporate America common to them as a group. Several years ago, I was invited to such a meeting at a local pub by a group of Christians from Target. We made a deal that they would buy me drinks and I would give them feedback on their questions and challenges.

We talked about several issues, among them the question of "bad goods." Two in particular were concerning to them: the increasing number of books and magazines that they described as "soft porn," and the sale of abortifacients and contraceptives at the pharmacy.

Target sells thousands of products and most of them are good goods, but some of what they provide, though increasingly acceptable in our society, would not be considered good by Christians. The thorny question thus arises: At what point can Christian employees cooperate with such evil without becoming evil themselves? At what point do they become complicit? Some in the group were also becoming uneasy over the public stances the company was taking over gay marriage, transgender policies, and the homosexual lifestyle.

The conversation raised an important but difficult distinction in moral theology between formal and material cooperation with evil. Because the world is fallen, and because Christians live in societies that are not fully Christian and are necessarily tied to various political, economic, and social networks in those societies, they are inevitably involved in morally imperfect situations. The only way to avoid this would be to segregate oneself completely from all connection to non-Christians, and even then, the problem would remain. So the question necessarily arises: When and how is it morally permissible to cooperate with evil, and when is it not? To note a few recent examples of the problem: during the 1930s, IBM, along with other US companies, had trade relations with Germany as the Nazis were taking power, and supplied them with the best instruments to maximize their destruction. Most people have come to think that this was a moral failure. In the 1970s and 80s, some companies refused to invest in South Africa under unjust apartheid, whereas others argued they would invest, but would do so in a way that could help change the system. How best to sort out what should be done?

The distinction between formal and material cooperation is easy to understand but often difficult to apply. A key to understanding the distinction hinges on the presence or absence of intention. To formally cooperate with evil means that one's intention is to perform the evil act. One shares not only in the act itself but also in the intention behind it. So, for example, if the Christian employees at Target were intentionally marketing soft porn and abortifacients, they would be in direct conflict with natural law and with their faith. They would be consciously intending things that were wrong. The principle in such a case is clear enough.

Things get muddier when we attempt to understand material cooperation with evil. Material cooperation shares in the act often in an indirect way, without sharing the intention. For instance, one pays taxes to a government that may use some portion of the funds for immoral acts. Or, one might purchase food from a grocery store that does not pay their employees a living wage. In these cases, there is no intention to accomplish the evil involved, so there is no formal cooperation with it. But there is material cooperation with it. Avoiding formal cooperation does not necessarily let us off the hook.

The employees I met with from Target did not market soft porn or contraceptives and abortifacients. Their work was in other parts of the business. But what made them uneasy was that these products were becoming increasingly present in the organization as a whole. What were they to do? Should they say nothing? Should they speak out, and if so, how? Should they start looking for different jobs?

As I discussed this unease with the Target employees, two issues became clear. The first was that the amount of revenue brought in by these products was minuscule compared to all the other products Target produced. And, second, none of these employees had any influence on what was being sold; they weren't in a position to do anything about it. As a result, none of them felt that leaving Target was necessary. They were not intending harm, the work they were doing was producing good goods, and although they wished Target would not produce bad products, their material cooperation in the evil involved was minimal.

In our conversation, we raised a different scenario to illustrate the point: If these employees did have influence, what would they say and do? One element of material cooperation with evil is that while one does not intend the evil involved, one should, if the possibility arose, limit or remove the evil. The employees gave good, reasonable arguments why Target should not carry soft porn. First, Target serves families, and in light of the number of children who come into the stores, the company should not expose children to such materials. Second, Target does not have to supply every product on the market. It can avoid cigarettes, pornography, violent video games, and so forth. Such products may have market value, in the sense that someone is willing to exchange money for them, but sometimes markets simply indicate that people's priorities are askew. Target is not under some legal obligation to carry such products. These arguments held the power to remind Target what it looks like when it is at its best. Such employees could work at Target, not intend such evil, and when opportunities arose, could exercise influence to mitigate the evil.

## CONCLUSION

Many of the students who speak with me about their future professional life want to create goods that are truly good and services that truly serve. We are *homo faber*, man the maker! We are made in the image of a God who is a Creator. We have an inherent desire to make things, to move things out of our head and into reality. Thomas Aquinas connects this creative desire to make to the virtue of magnificence, which in Latin combines the words *magna* (great) and *facere* (make)—"to make great things."[11] When we create goods and services for the purpose of benefitting others, we, in Thomas' words, "combine execution with greatness of purpose."[12] Our making as a virtue contributes to the good outside of us and to the character within us.

[11] Aquinas, *Summa theologiae* II, q. 134, a. 2.
[12] Aquinas, II-II, q. 128, a. 1.

CHAPTER 7

# Good Wealth
## Its Creation and Distribution

Twenty years ago, my mother died of cancer at the age of sixty-eight. Although it was a good death and a profound experience, it was also a very vulnerable and fragile time for our family. There were two institutions that supported and guided my father and siblings as we coped with the loss of my mother: our parish church with its pastor, Fr. Brankin, and the local Catholic hospital. While there were several people from the hospital who assisted us through this difficult time, Ruby, a hospice nurse's aid, stood out with great force.

Ruby cared for my mother during the final month of her life in our home. She was an African American Baptist woman who brought a tremendous amount of joy and consolation to my mother, a traditional Irish Catholic from County Offlay, Ireland.

Ruby came in three days a week to care for my mother, bathing her, changing the bed, messaging her ailing body, and lifting her spirits. She was a natural, both in terms of how she physically touched my mother and how she spiritually engaged her on her impending death. We would hear them laughing together, sharing stories of their children and talking about the Lord in their lives. Ecumenism was alive and well in that room. They would not have made much progress on doctrinal unity, but still, they witnessed a profound spiritual union.

Ruby's work was a great gift to our family, but there was a problem. She was not well-paid. As a nurse's aide for hospice work, she was one of lowest paid people in the health care industry. They say wages are like shoes: if they are too small, they gall and pinch us, but if they are too large they cause us to stumble and trip. As a single mother with a couple of children, life was not easy for Ruby. Her wages, despite her good work, were galling and pinching.

Ruby was paid according to market value but not according to justice. Many businesspeople and market economists cringe at such a statement. They say that the buying and selling of labor is the same as the buying and selling of any other commodity such as soy beans—its price determined by the interaction of supply and demand. If Ruby wanted to change her situation and get better pay, she should get the requisite skills and go into another profession.

In part, the economists are right. Ruby—like anyone who works within a market system—is subject to the forces of the market. For the most part, customers will only pay for the instrumental value of work, that is, they will not pay more than the value they receive for the products and services bought. If the hospital decided to pay Ruby and all the lowest-paid employees higher wages, it would most likely price itself out of the market.

Yet Ruby is one of millions of examples, showing us that markets cannot exhaust our understanding of how we pay people. A market produces a wage, but it cannot ensure the status of the wage's moral worth. Wages, like most things in life, can be either excessive or defective. A labor market that fails to value the physical and spiritual care of the dying enough to give its workers a living wage is defective, just as a labor market that values a man who can hit a little ball with a stick at millions of dollars is excessive.

The challenge is knowing how to respond to such excesses and defects. A wage that fails to meet the needs of a full-time adult employee will struggle to carry the weight of a real relationship between employee and employer. Yet to simply raise wages without implementing other changes would be self-defeating. Companies can find themselves at a competitive disadvantage if the labor costs are significantly higher than those of their competitors.

The last time I saw Ruby was at my mother's funeral. She was like an angel—a messenger from God—whose work offered consolation amidst the profound loss of our mother. There are millions of Rubys in the workforce today. Their labor meets the needs of others (good goods), but it does not provide for their own needs. Addressing the situations of the Rubys of the world is a multifaceted problem, but from a business perspective, a key factor is that the pay Ruby receives is dependent upon the wealth generated by the organization. It is precisely this relationship between the creation and distribution of wealth that gives us a clear understanding of good wealth.

It is not easy to pay just wages to people like Ruby, who are considered low-skilled, but the logic of exchange used by businesspeople and economists is too mechanical, too neat, and, frankly, too simplistic to deal with a case such as hers. On the other hand, if we perceive clearly the integral relationship between wealth creation and wealth distribution and the true sources of wealth, we can come to Ruby's situation with a deeper understanding of how an organization can create good wealth.

## GOOD WEALTH: CREATION
## AND DISTRIBUTION

Wealth cannot be distributed if it has not been created—nor should wealth be created without a just distribution of it to those responsible for its creation. These two dimensions of good wealth, creation and distribution, which are too often placed in opposition to one another, cannot be understood apart from each other. They are like two sides of a coin.

In terms of wealth creation, business enterprises are the economic engine of society. As a creator of products and services (good goods) and jobs (good work), businesses must exercise the stewardship of their resources such that they create more than they have been given. Good stewards of wealth are those who not only take from creation's abundance but also contribute to it. In business, such stewardship demands a great deal of frugality and economic discipline, requiring that one carefully track costs and revenue, drive out waste, improve production processes, deliver on time, and enhance quality.

When a business generates more than what has been given to it, we call the result profit or margin, a surplus of retained earnings over expenses. This profit enables a company to sustain itself into the future. Profits wisely used over time create equity in companies, which strengthens the firm's wealth-generating capacities to build for the future. A business with a healthy balance sheet, for example, is better able to build a secure future than those laden with debt. A profitable business creates the conditions for well-paying jobs, opportunities for employee development, useful products and services, satisfied customers, and vibrant communities.

Yet, as we pointed out in chapter four, profit is like food. We need it if we are to be healthy and sustained in life, but we ought not to live for it. It is a means, not an end, a reward, not a motive, which, incidentally, is why so many executive incentive programs can be so destructive. As we have said before, profit makes a good servant, but a lousy master.

Wealth creation, however, is only one side of the coin. We also need to speak of wealth distribution and, in particular, the just distribution of wealth. Without profit, a company dies, but without a just distribution of wealth, a business is no more than legally organized robbery. This kind of banditry can be seen in practices such as price gouging and fixing, erecting monopolies, hoarding benefits, overpaying executives, shifting costs onto the poor and to future generations, refusing to pay suppliers or maintaining unreasonable extensions of payments, corporate welfare and wage theft, and, unfortunately, the list goes on.

Too often, however, a just distribution of resources is seen as only a political function through regulations and taxation, dependent only upon governmental legal systems for regulation. Such a view ignores an important role of business—the task of establishing right relationships, which is the meaning of justice. The Latin root of justice is *ius,* meaning "right," and in particular, "right relation-

ships." In the Old Testament the Hebrew words *mišpāt*
(justice) and *ṣĕdāqâ* (righteousness) describe the fulfillment of responsibilities between employer and employee,
ruler and subjects, God and His people, husband and wife,
parent and child.

As it relates to business, a just distribution calls for
wealth to be allocated in a way that creates "right relationships" with those who have participated in the creation of
the wealth. This practice of the virtue of justice raises a
set of knotty and enduring moral challenges for business
leaders. Among other things, businesses need to discern
and account for the moral implications of how they allo-
cate resources to employees (a just wage and compensation
as well as possibilities of employee ownership), to customers (just prices), to owners (fair returns), to suppliers (just
prices and fair terms on receivables), to government (just
tax payments), to the larger community, and especially to
the poor (philanthropy).

Pius XII compared the place of wealth in human society to the function of blood in the human body: it needs
to circulate to all the parts in order to make the whole
healthy.[1] Good wealth depends not only on its creation
but also on its just distribution. Where there is a con-

---

[1] Pius XII, *Dilecti filii*, letter to the German Bishops, October 18, 1949, quoted in Jean-Yves Calvez and Jacques Perrin, *The Church and Social Justice: The Social Teachings of the Popes from Leo XIII to Pius XII* (Chicago: Henry Regnery, 1961), 149.

centration of wealth in a few hands, there is most likely a "blood clot" causing disease. Business plays an essential role in creating a just distribution of wealth that both generates authentic prosperity and alleviates debilitating poverty. When there is excessive inequality or a too great distance between rich and poor, businesses, regions, and whole countries become ripe for increasing violence, greater crime, and possible revolution. Business can be a leader in fostering right relationships and mitigating economic inequities, thus furthering social peace.

If we are to understand good wealth and its dynamic of creation and distribution, and in particular, how the Rubys of the world can be treated with justice, we need to better understand the *sources* of good wealth and how they relate to the idea of the logic of gift.

## SOURCES OF GOOD WEALTH RECEIVED: NATURE AND CULTURE

While businesses create and distribute wealth, they are first given wealth in multiple ways. We too often think of the entrepreneur as the person who creates wealth *ex nihilo*—out of nothing. The folk lore of the self-made entrepreneur is simply an illusion. Only God creates *ex nihilo*; entrepreneurs must first receive. Their activity is humbler than they might like to think: they are co-creators. The two most significant gifts they receive and by which they co-create are the natural world and the family. If they fail to recognize these gifts, crisis usually follows. Ignoring the logic of gift—the logic of giving and receiving—does not result in our breaking that logical necessity. It breaks us.

Take, for example, the environmental crisis, which we discussed in chapter six. The most basic gift we inherit is our natural environment. Without the goods of creation, we are bankrupt. We have become increasingly aware—though not as quickly as we should—of the demands of proper stewardship of the environment. The Book of Genesis tells us to "till and keep" creation (Gen 2:15), but we have tended to "till too much and keep too little."[2]

It is true that nature does not give out its wealth without human work, human creativity, and human ingenuity. Yet, while much of the wealth of our economy comes from the knowledge of workers, businesses are always beholden to the gifts of the natural world and of the land.

The other crisis facing us is the crisis of marriage and family. When we praise leaders for their work ethic, we are often indirectly praising their parents. We stand on the shoulders of our families who have done far more than we know to get us to where we are. Marriage and family provide people with the social conditions for their proper

---

[2] See Cardinal Peter Turkson, "Protect the Earth, Dignify Humanity: The Moral Dimensions of Climate Change and Sustainable Development," (address, Vatican City, April 28, 2015), http://www.casinapioiv.va/content/dam/accademia/pdf/turkson.pdf. See also Francis, Encyclical Letter on Care for Our Common Home *Laudato si'* (May 24, 2015), §37.

development. The family is an institution that fosters the common good.

As mentioned in chapter four on the common good, families are a primary institution within society. They create enduring relationships that mutually support their members, especially during difficult times. They bond people together. They enlarge the capacity of their members to make sacrifices. Despite all the challenges of family life, families tend to provide the stability that supports political and educational institutions, all of which influences the development of an economic system. Yet, as several scholars have noted, the social dynamics of family life are too often ignored or discounted by those who speak about the economic health of society, and in particular, of business.[3]

The relationship between marriage and wealth creation and distribution is revealed by a significant fault line. In the aggregate, those who marry and stay married have much better material and emotional lives than those who do not marry or whose marriages have failed. Of course there are exceptions to this. There are couples who stay in marriages that are stale and abusive and there are single parents who live heroic and holy lives, but in the aggregate these are exceptions not the rule. "Evidence is mounting," Pope Francis tells us, "that the decline of

---

[3]  See Charles Murray, *Coming Apart: the State of White America, 1960–2010* (New York: Crown Forum, 2012).

the marriage culture is associated with increased poverty and a host of other social ills, disproportionately affecting women, children, and the elderly."[4] The decline of a marriage culture and the resulting increase in poverty points to the relationship between *economic* and *cultural* poverty and inequality. The poor are not only impoverished materially, but also institutionally.[5]

For example, there is an increasing cultural divide between lower and middle class populations who are withdrawing from marriage and religion, and upper-middle class populations who have higher participation rates in such primary institutions.[6] While marriage and religious participation rates declined for all classes since the 1960s, significant divergence between classes started to occur in the 1980s.

---

[4] Francis, "We Must Foster a New Human Ecology" (address, Humanum Conference, November 17, 2014), Vatican website, http://w2.vatican.va/content/francesco/en/speeches/2014/november/documents/papa-francesco_20141117_congregazione-dottrina-fede.html.

[5] See Federal Reserve Bank of St. Louis and the Board of Governors of the Federal Reserve System, eds., *Economic Mobility: Research & Ideas on Strengthening Families, Communities & the Economy*, https://www.stlouisfed.org/community-development/publications/economic-mobility.

[6] Faith institutions complement families by becoming a family of families that support one another in times of crisis. W. Bradford Wilcox, Andrew J. Cherlin, Jeremy E. Uecker, and Matthew Messel, "No Money, No Honey, No Church: The Deinstitutionalization of Religious Life Among the White Working Class," *Research in the Sociology of Work* 23 (2012): 227–250. See also Amy L. Wax, "Engines of Inequality: Class, Race and Structure," *Family Law Quarterly* 41, no. 3 (2007): 567, http://lsr.nellco.org/cgi/viewcontent.cgi?article=1219&context=upenn_wps.

For the upper-middle class, marriage stabilized during the mid-1980s, and since then, actual divorce rates have started to decline for this group.[7] For the lower to middle classes, however, marriage participation rates have continued to slide to the point that now only a minority are married, and a majority of children have no fathers at home. Whereas in the 1960s both the poor and the rich participated in religion and marriage at similar rates, today the trends look different: a majority of upper-middle class people marry, most of their children are born into two-parent homes, and they usually attend religious services; a majority of middle to lower class people do not marry, most of their children are born into single-parent homes, and they usually do not attend religious services.[8]

As the "marrying rich" and "unmarrying poor" move in opposite directions, the traditional working class is slowly unraveling, its members deprived of the economic

[7] W. Bradford Wilcox and Elizabeth Marquardt, eds., "When Marriage Disappears: The New Middle America," *The State of Our Unions: Marriage in America* (2010), http://stateofourunions.org/2010/SOOU2010.pdf.

[8] See Murray, *Coming Apart*. See also Reuben Finighan and Robert Putnam, "A Country Divided: The Growing Opportunity Gap in America," in *Economic Mobility: Research & Ideas on Strengthening Families, Communities & the Economy*, ed. Federal Reserve Bank of St. Louis and the Board of Governors of the Federal Reserve System, 145., https://www.stlouisfed.org/~/media/Files/PDFs/Community-Development/EconMobilityPapers/Section2/EconMobility_2-2FinighanPutnam_508.pdf?la=en.

mobility they once enjoyed.[9] Not only are they increasingly opting out of marriage and family, they are increasingly opting out of full-time employment.[10] The poor are not only economically poor; they are culturally and institutionally poor. They have become isolates, disconnected from the common bonds of family, faith, work, education, and politics.[11] The United States has changed from a society with great economic mobility to one with very little. The poor stay poor and rich stay rich. Increasingly, a culture of poverty seeps in, creating greater class conflict, such that society, in Charles Murray's phrase, looks to be "coming apart."

It is true of course that the relationships between family and wealth distribution are complex. On one hand, as manufacturing jobs moved abroad in the 1970s and 80s, lower and middle class workers without a college degree found fewer economic opportunities. The impact of globalization, the decline of unions, and automation, as well as other factors, are all part of complex web that make life harsh and difficult. But broken families with fatherless

[9] See Erika Bachiochi, "The Family: Between Personal Rights and Social Needs," *Mirror of Justice* (blog), http://mirrorofjustice.blogs.com/mirrorofjustice/2017/04/reflections-on-my-time-in-rome-as-a-speaker-at-the-conference-commemorating-popularum-progressio.html.

[10] See Murray, *Coming Apart*, chap. 9.

[11] See R. R. Reno, *Resurrecting the Idea of a Christian Society* (Washington, DC: Regnery Faith, 2016), 49.

homes, out-of-wedlock births, cohabitation, and no-fault divorce tends to bring about a weak family institution with few protective resources to deal with adverse economic and political forces.

## BACK TO RUBY AND GOOD WEALTH

So, what does all this mean for the Rubys of the world and their organizations? I want to highlight two implications. First, concerning wealth creation, time has shown that new jobs, which are critical to the health of a business sector, usually come not from well-established companies but from entrepreneurial start-ups—small and medium-sized companies, especially family businesses.[12] New businesses need entrepreneurs who are willing to take risks, who have faith in a future, who have access to credit, and who can operate in a reasonable regulatory environment.

While the macroeconomic environment plays an important role here, so does family structure. Entrepreneurship, and in particular family businesses, is dependent upon healthy families. One study has shown that young adults who grow up in intact families work at least 156 more hours per year than their peers from single-parent families. The authors of the study explain that "this body of research underlines that strong families provide an ideal environment for acquiring the skills and habits needed

---

[12] Small Business & Entrepreneurship Council, "Facts & Data on Small Business and Entrepreneurship," http://sbecouncil.org/about-us/facts-and-data/.

to thrive in the contemporary free market."[13] Intact marriages and healthy families simply have greater capacity to teach virtues such as justice and courage, diligence and industriousness—so needed for success in life—than those of broken or non-existent marriages.[14]

Here we run up against some difficult realities. As wonderful as Ruby is in her work and as a person, she has not developed the skills necessary to get better pay. Her education was poor. She comes from a broken family. She is a single parent. And she has few familial resources to draw upon when things don't go well. All of these conditions have reduced Ruby's wealth-creating capabilities. None of these conditions were caused by her employer, and for the most part Ruby did not create her cultural context.

Yet, even though the hospital is not responsible for Ruby's lack of skills and poor education, it is responsible for the nature of its relationship with Ruby. And though

---

[13] W. Bradford Wilcox reports that the shift in family structure away from marriage accounts for approximately forty percent of the increase in economic inequality since 1975. For example, children from lower to middle income, married, two-parent families have greater economic mobility than those raised without both parents or whose parents are unmarried. For further information, see Wilcox's studies with The University of Virginia's National Marriage Project, http://nationalmarriageproject.org/.

[14] The witness of many single parents who overcome their situations and raise beautiful and vibrant children is moving, but the aggregate data reveals that without an intact two-parent, committed marriage, the chances of poverty, family disintegration, abuse, and the continuation of this cycle increases significantly.

Ruby is not fully responsible for her situation, she has a
job where she can influence the future. This brings us to
our second point on wealth distribution. When an employer receives work from an employee, both participate
not only in an economic exchange but also in a personal
relationship. This relationship, if it is to be just, has three
convictions that should guide the creation and distribution
of wealth: need, contribution, and order.

- Need: For a relationship to flourish in business,
  an employer must recognize that employees, by
  their labor, "surrender" their time and energy
  and cannot use them for other purposes. A living
  wage, then, is the minimum amount due to every
  independent wage earner by the mere fact that
  he or she is a human being with a life to maintain and a family to support. A wage that fails
  to meet the needs of an employee (in particular,
  a full-time adult) is a wage that will struggle to
  carry the weight of a real relationship.
- Contribution: While the principle of need is
  necessary for determining a just wage, it is in-
  sufficient on its own, since it only accounts for
  the consumptive needs of employees and does
  not factor in their productive contributions to
  the organization. Because of effort and sacrifice
  as well as skill, education, experience, scarcity

of talent, and decision-making ability, some employees contribute more to the organization than others, and are therefore due more pay. An equitable wage, then, is the contribution of an employee's productivity and effort within the context of the existing amount of profits and resources of the organization.

- Order: Pay is not only income for the worker; it is also a cost to the employer, a cost that impacts significantly the economic order of the organization. Without proper evaluation of the way a living and equitable wage will affect the economic order of an organization, the notion of a just wage becomes no more than a high-sounding moralistic impracticality. A sustainable wage, then, is the organization's ability to pay wages that are sustainable for the economic health of the organization as a whole.

In Ruby's case, a tension exists between the principle of need and the principle of order. Raising Ruby's wages could put the economic sustainability of the hospital at risk. The key to resolving the tension is invoking the principle of contribution. Three conditions of relationship are necessary to come to a fruitful resolution.

First, hospital administrators in this case must resist the common practice of passively delegating their responsibilities simply to the mechanical force of labor markets. As managers, they are moral agents, distributors of justice, and not mere market technicians.

Second, Ruby has to take responsibility for the fact that she does not have the skills to warrant enough wealth to pay her a living wage. Whatever the circumstances that got her there, she is the one who needs to enhance her skill level. The hospital may be able to help with this. The state may develop skill-based programs for under-skilled employees. Manufacturing companies, for example, will have assemblers take courses at local community colleges to prepare them to be manufacturing technicians. Not only is this a great growth opportunity for them, but better skills lead to increased productivity, which then leads to higher wages. In addition, companies can receive grants from the state to cover the educational costs of training employees. The state has an interest in keeping manufacturing jobs.

Third, hospital administrators should realize that every action has a reaction, and that raising wage levels without changing the work process would have serious consequences on overall cost structure. To simply pour surplus profits into wages without any consideration as to how the performance of the organization might be strengthened would undermine the hospital's ability to pay sustainable living wages.

What should become clear to the hospital administration is that low wages are merely a symptom of a much larger problem of how the organization structures the work itself. When work is designed to use a wage rate below a living wage, it is difficult to pay a person like Ruby anything more than what she is receiving now, regardless of her talents. Good wealth is dependent upon good work. Prudence dictates that the living wage cannot come about automatically. It has to come through redesigning the work and giving workers skills. If administrators are going to raise labor rates to pay a living wage, they need to find ways to reduce their labor costs.

It is important to recognize that the relationship between Ruby and the hospital is a two-way interaction. The hospital is not responsible for paying employees more than a sustainable wage (a wage consistent with the sound financial management of the firm), even if that wage falls below a living wage. To do so would unjustly place the hospital—and all the firm's employees—at risk of economic failure. In a market economy, no organization can be obligated to pay without regard to the effect of labor costs on its competitive position, since that would amount to an imprudent choice, leading possibly to economic failure for the business. To "impose justice" in this manner is doomed to long-term failure.

Nevertheless, the hospital administrators have a moral obligation to create right relationships with Ruby and other employees and to work *toward* a living wage. Ruby also needs to take responsibility for her situation and work toward gaining the necessary skills to make a living wage. Ruby is not merely a recipient of justice but also an integral part of the process of creating right relationships, which depends on how she chooses to pursue her work. Employees have a responsibility to develop their knowledge and skills—not only to increase their pay—but also to improve the competitiveness of the organization. If they don't continuously learn and develop in their work, they fail to give their company its just due, and instead, they contribute to attitudes of employee entitlement.

## CONCLUSION: A WARNING ON WEALTH FIXATION

Our focus on Ruby has brought out only one aspect of creating and distributing wealth, but it is an important and, in many respects, a foundational aspect. Not to pay a living wage when an employee's full-time hours are necessary for them to earn a living, no matter how beautiful the work may be, will eventually strain the relationship between employer and employee and undermine what makes for good wealth.

Good wealth, like all the goods of business, and the common good itself, is predicated on just relationships. One of the corrupting influences within business is a fixation on "maximizing wealth," whether in the form of shareholder wealth, profit, or margins. When wealth maximization is the principal motive of business leaders and owners, employees begin to adopt a similar motive—that of wage maximization. Once these two competitive attitudes have developed, the possibility of getting to the deeper relationships between employee and employer vanish. Profits and wages alone do not have the capacity to bind people together in a way that enables them to flourish.

Imagine what would have happened if Ruby decided to calibrate her quality of work according to the money she was paid. "The hospital gives me little pay, therefore, I will give minimal service." If Ruby had seen her work as just a job, and the hospital had paid her simply as a market activity, the relationship would have been thin, and the care of my mother would have been cheapened. This "maximizing and exchange" mentality fails to produce good wealth. Maximizing mentalities of profits and wages can only be allocated and not participated in. It is when persons participate in a deeper good that real relationships create the flourishing of people. My family was blessed by Ruby because she saw her work not as a job but a vocation. She met our needs in a profound way. The hope is that the hospital might find a way to pay her and meet *her* needs.

# III. LEISURE

·✥·

# CHAPTER 8

# THE POWER OF SUNDAY: HOLY REST[1]

WE began this book by speaking of the roots of faith, which are necessary to live out the Gospel in our work. We covered work themes such as vocation, the common good, subsidiarity, the subjective dimension of work, the universal destination of material goods, and justice—all of which form the roots one needs to be faithful at work. But now we move to and conclude with the deepest roots of leisure found in contemplation, holiness and above all worship.

We cannot simply achieve our vocation. We need to receive it, and this is why we need Christ, the Church, and, perhaps surprisingly, Sunday—the Sabbath. Sunday is a day of worship, rest, of celebration, of receptivity. It

[1] This book is dedicated to my wife, Teresa, but this chapter has been particularly inspired by her insight and practice of Sunday, by which our family has been particularly blessed.

has been said that "More than the Jewish People have kept the Sabbath, the Sabbath has kept the Jews."[2] The same can be said for Christians. More than Christians keeping their Sunday obligation, the Lord's Day has kept the Church.

"If you want to kill Christianity," it has been said, "you must abolish Sunday."[3] Things can be abolished in multiple ways. Romano Guardini speaks about how certain economic and social forces constantly shove Sunday aside. He writes, "Work gnaws at it; amusement elbows its way into it, crowding out holiness; the significance of keeping holy is misunderstood, and rest is imposed with a resultant boredom that is worse than if work had continued."[4] Through overfull sports schedules, mindless amusements, the ubiquity of screens that never shut off, and the habit of viewing Sunday as a mop-up day from the previous week's activities, the Sabbath loses power to recreate and renew our relationship with the Lord and with others.

Christians, in particular, can too easily dismiss the Third Commandment, "Keep Holy the Sabbath." If we violated the commandment about adultery the way we typically violate the

---

[2]  This saying is commonly attributed to the Jewish writer Ahad Ha'am.

[3]  Supposedly Voltaire stated this, but I cannot find the reference. It does seem in keeping with his thought, and with that of all the French revolutionaries whom he so strongly influenced. They did in fact abolish Sunday—or at least attempted to do so.

[4]  Romano Guardini, *Meditations Before Mass* (Notre Dame, IN: Ave Maria Press, 2014), 55.

command for keeping the Sabbath, we would see more clearly the wreckage it causes. "Honey, I tried not committing adultery this week, but it didn't quite work; but I will try again next week." No marriage would last long under such circumstances. The Sabbath—the commandment to both rest and celebrate—is essential to our work and to the order of our lives.

Thus we come back to the place from which we started our discussion, with the question, "What do we rest in?" The power of Sunday, the Lord's Day, the Sabbath, is found in its potential for keeping us free: Sunday is the day when production, consumption, and especially technology do not own us; when we are defined not by our doing or having, but by our being made in God's image; when we remember that life is a gift given, not a task achieved. Sunday helps us to see and to maintain our true identity. If we do not get Sunday right, we will not get Monday right.

The importance of the Sabbath and my need for Sunday became clear to me in 1999. Ironically, it was the year I received my first sabbatical (a word with the same root as Sabbath, which means "to rest") at the University of St. Thomas. My sabbatical was anything but an experience of rest: gutting the upstairs of our dilapidated house, running a major international conference in India, finishing a book. Although my routine changed that year, my habits of overworking were much the same. But this was soon to change.

That year I was asked to give a paper at an academic

conference in San Francisco. Immediately before presenting the paper, I was struck by an anxiety attack that challenged my ability to *do* in a way I had ever before experienced. My breath seemed to fail me, and as much as I tried, I could not muster the will power to overcome this sudden inability to speak in public.

I was on the verge of leaning over to my introducer to tell him I could not give my presentation and looking for the nearest exit. But I was too late. He began his introduction, and my panic grew worse. Now I had to talk. Just say one word, I thought to myself, then the next, then the next. As I spoke, my voice quivered, and I had to deliver the words slowly, fearing that I would lose my ability to speak, as if the oxygen in my lungs were running out. It was one of the most humbling, perhaps even humiliating, experiences of my professional life.

The event left me feeling vulnerable. I began to search for the cause of this anxiety, this threat to my *doing*. Was it a physical problem? Was I drinking too much coffee? Not getting enough sleep? Working too hard? Was it a spiritual problem? Was I becoming too arrogant in what I was doing? Was the Lord teaching me a lesson in humility? In my anxiety, my mind whirled from one possible explanation to the next.

During the same year, Teresa and I were becoming increasingly aware of the importance of Sunday and its

Sabbath role, as we prepared for the Jubilee Year in 2000. Up to that time, Sunday was for us a different kind of day, but not a special day. It was different because of our pattern of going to church, making a mid-morning brunch, and watching or playing a sport in the afternoon. But it was not a day of rest. Even worse, Sundays tended to bring along a rather depressing feeling that set in especially in the late afternoon or early evening. I would find myself in a funk, experiencing a certain low-grade depression, a feeling of emptiness, and lack of meaning.

Hoping to change all that, Teresa and I made a commitment in 1999 not to work on Sundays. I would stop working in the morning before the kids were up, and both of us would set aside house projects that we did not get to during the week. I distinctly remember the feeling of that first Sunday. It was like Christmas morning.

Sunday mornings have now become the most powerful time of the week for us. Setting aside the weekly Sabbath time has made our marriage better and stronger; I would even go so far to say that it has saved our marriage. Our relationships with our children are richer, and our relationships with God are more personal, even in the midst of family struggles and our own continuing immaturities.

On the other six days of the week, when I wake up, my work is waiting for me—sometimes actually pressing down on me. But on Sunday mornings, what awaits me is rest; not only a rest from work, but a rest in a reality that is beyond my doings and achievements, a rest that is asking me to receive reality rather than to change it. Most deeply, it is a resting in Christ.

I wish I could say that because of my Sunday observance I no longer get nervous before talks, that I never get depressed on Sunday afternoons, that our family Sabbath time is a continual experience of harmonious bliss, but this would not be true. The world is still fallen, and I am still battling sin. In keeping with its very nature, the Sabbath command is not simply instrumental, its goodness or usefulness to be measured by my success in various aspects of life.

Yet I do think that even if keeping the Sabbath has not made me more productive, it has made me more perceptive in my work. And though our children sometimes think we are obsessive about keeping away from screens and shopping on the Lord's Day, it has made our family stronger. These are the fruits of keeping the Sabbath, but they are not where its main power lies.

The power of Sunday can be best expressed when Augustine writes in the first paragraph in the *Confessions,* "You stir in man to take pleasure in praising you, because you have made us for yourself, and our heart is restless until it rests in you."[5] The power of Sunday is in the rest

---

[5] Augustine, *Confessions,* trans. Henry Chadwick (Oxford: Oxford University Press, 1991), I, chap. 1, §1.

it provides, not the work it produces; in receptivity, not in activity; in its celebratory affirmation of the deeply ordered goodness of creation, all of which nurtures our relationship with Christ. Its power is in moving us from a focus on ability, talent, achievement, and calculating results, and toward the healthy and necessary realization of what is done to and for us—all that can only be received and accepted—and ultimately toward the grace that points us to what is authentically human, to who we should be. It is a holy time, not for us to work on things but for God to work on us. Sunday reveals the heart of the logic of gift that has been expressed throughout this book.

There are many challenges arising from our current culture that make it difficult to implement and experience the potency of Sunday, some of which we explored in chapter two. Here we will confront the "problem of the weekend" before moving on to the cultivation of Sabbath habits and to a discussion of specific Sunday practices that can unleash the power of Sunday and deepen our vision and commitment to good work.

## THE PROBLEM OF THE WEEKEND

Stephen Covey wrote an excellent book entitled *Seven Habits of Highly Effective People*. It has sold over twenty-five million copies in forty languages and is considered one of the most influential leadership books ever written. There are many good points in Covey's treatment; but the seventh habit, which he calls, "sharpen the saw," helps us to see a particular problem. According to this rendering, we rest from our work in order to become more productive, to increase our capacity to handle challenges, to recharge ourselves so that we can achieve success. All of this is true, but the danger is that this can create a state of mind that never leaves work. All time is ordered to work time, for we cannot abide in rest without worrying about whether it serves the next moment's occupation. This does not create rest; it tends instead toward anxiety.

Describing this anxiety, the Hungarian psychologist Sándor Ferenczi coined the term "Sunday Neurosis." Why is it, he wondered, that when we take time to rest, we find often that we quickly become restless? We experience dis-ease and angst that often begins on Sunday afternoon. It expresses itself in terms of a lack of a sense of meaning in life, an emptiness, a listless boredom, often a low-grade depression, and a generally melancholy spirit.

The reason for this experience may have to do with the way we work, but it usually has more to do with the way we practice leisure. Our rest often results in restlessness precisely because our leisure time lacks spiritual enrichment connected to the habits of silence, celebration, and fraternal charity—habits that we will explore in the next section. When we lose touch with a spiritual and communal form of leisure, we instrumentalize our rest—that is, we don't do it for itself but for some utilitarian benefit. T.S. Eliot once wrote, "The last temptation is the greatest treason; to do the right deed for the wrong reason."[6] If I am nice to my wife simply because I want to get things from her, I begin to corrupt our love. There are things we not only need to do, but also need to do for the right reasons. One of these is the way we spend our leisure time.

While the weekend is crucial for our rest, without spiritual forms of leisure, especially worship, we lose sight of authentic celebrations and of the good that is affirmed in our celebrations. In a letter entitled "The Lord's Day" (*Dies Domini*), John Paul II explained, "When Sunday loses its fundamental meaning and becomes merely part of a 'weekend,' it can happen that people stay locked within a horizon so limited that they can no longer see 'the heavens.' Hence, although ready to celebrate, they are really incapable of doing so."[7]

Our need is not for just any kind of leisure, but for the kind of celebration that radically affirms the goodness of the world and that marvels at what God has created.[8] If our weekends and holidays become filled with frenetic amusements, we will miss out on the meaning of celebration and lose sight of the deeper reality of the world that can be received only in contemplation. It is crucial that we develop spiritual

---

[6] T. S. Eliot, *Murder in the Cathedral* (New York: Harcourt, Brace & World, 1935), 44.

[7] John Paul II, *Dies Domini*, §4.

[8] John Paul II, *Dies Domini*, §17.

habits with the power to move us to this deeper reality.

## THE LORD'S DAY:
## THREE ESSENTIAL HABITS

For Sunday to unleash its power for us, we will want to develop habits (virtues) that allow us to participate in its graces—habits of leisure, of receptivity that foster a contemplative outlook and help us to receive the world. Especially for businesspeople and leaders of organizations, habits of receptivity can be difficult to develop.

I saw these habits powerfully displayed in a good friend who was diagnosed with Parkinson's disease. In his late 50s, he was teaching, researching, and in the middle of writing a book. When he turned 60 all of these things were taken from him. But when I visited him, I was moved to find that there was no bitterness or sense of victimization in him. His life of receptivity prepared him to receive his illness.

### The first habit: silence

The first habit is that of silence and solitude, entailing not only turning off the noises around us but also quieting the emotions and thoughts that play within us. When these interior noises are not silenced, they result in illusion: visions of my own grandeur, perhaps feelings of the unappreciated genius, imagined debate scenarios with my nemesis where I win every time, or false heroism hinging on unlikely opportunities.

The internal recordings that we play over and over often mask the conditions of our reality and create a false image of ourselves. They prevent us from internal silence and deep rest; they form the monologue that perpetuates the restlessness of our restless hearts. As Benedict XVI provocatively put it, "Only if it is born from the silence of contemplation can our words have some value and usefulness, and not resemble the inflated discourses of the world that seek the consensus of public opinion."[9] Our silence purifies our thoughts and our words.

Sunday is meant to be a day that fosters silence. If we cannot find time for silence and solitude on Sunday, it will be difficult to find it anywhere else. Sunday is usually the day when the habit of silence can begin to take root. Pope Francis explains that "without prolonged moments of adoration, of prayerful encounter with the word, of sincere conversation with the Lord, our work easily becomes meaningless; we lose energy as a result of weariness and difficulties, and our fervour dies out."[10] Without a deep

---

[9] Benedict XVI, "Address of His Holiness Benedict XVI at the Beginning of the Academic Year of the Pontifical Roman Universities," October 23, 2006, https://w2.vatican.va/content/benedict-xvi/en/speeches/2006/october/documents/hf_ben-xvi_spe_20061023_anno-accademico.html. See also Robert Cardinal Sarah with Nicolas Diat, *The Power of Silence: Against the Dictatorship of Noise*, trans. Michael Miller (San Francisco: Ignatius Press, 2017).

[10] Francis, *Evangelii gaudium*, §62. See also the Dicastery for Promoting Integral Human Development, *Vocation of the Business Leader*, §§21, 70.

well of spiritual contemplation and reflection to draw upon, it is hard to see, for example, how business leaders can resist the negative dimensions of information technology that drive speed and efficiency at the expense of thoughtful reflection, patience, justice, and practical wisdom.

## The second habit: celebration

One of the deep challenges we have addressed throughout this book is that we value only the useful and not the good. This is a sign of disordered celebrations. Authentic celebrations are a means of participation in the revelatory insight that all God's creation is good. To authentically celebrate, we need to radically affirm the goodness of what we are celebrating. The celebratory dimension of a festival is the time to see and to affirm our end as good and not only useful. That sight, gained in celebration, can then penetrate ordinary reality.

Our cultural celebrations have significantly lost the deep spiritual roots that marked them as "holidays"—holy days. Consider the commercialization of Christmas, the decadence of Mardi Gras and St. Patrick's Day, the trivialization of Easter, the ghoulishness of Halloween. Our celebrations increasingly miss the main point of the feast: the affirmation of what is good and holy—the Resurrection (Easter and funerals), the Incarnation (Christmas), creative love (the marriage ceremony), and the coming of new life (Baptism). Such feasts, when authentically celebrated, have the potent capacity to re-create us and remind us of where we have come from, where we are going, and who we are.

However much the authenticity of our celebrations has suffered during the last thirty years, the Sunday Sabbath is still a powerful sign for our market economy that production and consumption do not own us. Sunday provides one of the few times and spaces in which the person is not defined principally as a worker or a consumer, but as a human, as a person who has been created and redeemed. Being reduced to only a worker or consumer dehumanizes us, since working and consuming can only preoccupy us toward limited ends. The Sabbath—authentically practiced—humanizes us and helps us to receive and affirm our true end.

The celebration of The Lord's Day is a feast day, a holy day, God's day, when we receive through Word and Sacrament the meaning of our existence, and that includes our work activity. To celebrate is essentially to worship, to proclaim what is most worthy. This means that worship is not an escape from the world, "rather it is the arrival at a vantage point from which we can see more deeply into the reality of the world."[11]

The sacramental, incarnational view of worship re-

---

[11] Alexander Schmemann, *For the Life of the World* (New York: St. Vladimir's Seminary Press, 1973), 27, quoted in Joseph Woodill, "Virtue Ethics: An Orthodox Appreciation," *Thought* 67, no. 2 (June 1992): 186.

veals that the spiritual illuminates the material, grace perfects nature, and worship makes one's work holy. For many Christians, the Eucharist reveals most deeply and most profoundly "the work of human hands" as the bread and wine are transformed into the real presence of Christ's body and blood, a presence that has the power to redeem the world.

Sundays, along with weddings, baptisms, funerals, and other such forms of celebratory leisure, invite us to a practice of festivity that "draws glory and exaltation from the past, not merely as reflected history, but by virtue of a historical reality *still operative in the present*."[12] In the Eucharist, for example, the past is not simply an isolated chronological moment, and nor is the future kingdom of God something simply to be awaited as we muddle through history. In the Eucharist, past and future converge, and Christ along with the whole Church is present. Eternity breaks upon time, and the mind and soul are brought to the deepest activity of celebration and worship: receptivity to the infinite, to God.[13]

## The third habit: charity

The practice of service to others, of going to the margins, is intimately tied to the habit of the Sabbath. Jesus of-

[12] Josef Pieper, "What is a Feast," in *Josef Pieper: An Anthology* (San Francisco: Ignatius Press, 1981), 153 (emphasis added).
[13] William Cavanaugh, *Torture and Eucharist: Theology, Politics, and the Body of Christ* (Oxford: Blackwell Publishing, 1998).

ten healed on the Sabbath and continues to do so. If the Sabbath is truly working within us, if deep silence and joyful celebration is awakening the fire of charity within us, we will become ever more sensitive to those who suffer around us, those who are ill, lonely, or marginalized.

As Sunday nurtures the faith, the faithful "look around to find people who may need their help. It may be that in their neighborhood or among those they know there are sick people, elderly people, children or immigrants who precisely on Sundays feel more keenly their isolation, needs and suffering."[14] Instead of being dominated by amusements, Sunday can become "a great school of charity" that deepens a disciplined sensitivity to the needs of others.[15]

Unlike the other two habits we have discussed, the habit of charity can seem more like work than like leisure. Yet the encounter with those who, at least on the surface of things, cannot do anything for us can be a most profound experience of receptivity. Jean Vanier, founder of the L'Arche Community, wrote that "if we remain at the level of 'doing' something for people, we can stay behind our barriers of superiority."[16] We share life most deeply with people when we are simply "with" them, especially those who are most vulnerable and marginalized.[17] It is often those who cannot seem to give us anything who, para-

---

[14] John Paul II, *Dies Domini*, §§72–73.

[15] John Paul II, *Dies Domini*.

[16] Jean Vanier, *Community and Growth* (New York: Paulist Press, 1989), 186.

[17] Vanier, *Community and Growth*

doxically, do more for us than we can do for them. As Benedict XVI has noted, "Those who are in a position to help others will realize that in doing so, they themselves *receive* help; being able to help others in no merit or achievement of their own. This duty is grace."[18]

## LORD'S DAY PRACTICES

What do these habits concretely look like on a Sunday? How can Sunday be a special day, a different kind of day? How can we mark it as a day of rest and celebration in the Lord?

There is no simple formula for developing the essential Sabbath habits, given the differences in circumstances and state of life in which we find ourselves. Still, we will want to find ways to institutionalize and ritualize the above three habits if we are to bring the power of the Sabbath into our lives. If we don't consciously make space for them, the default response of the culture will take over, and we will find ourselves wallowing in a bland day of amusements and activities that fail to recreate. Here are some ways our family has tried to institutionalize Sabbath practices, although never perfectly and always needing our attention to keep them fresh.

**1. Preparation during the Week:** As with most people, if our family does not carve out time for something and plan it out, it doesn't happen. My wife has a regular

---

[18] Benedict XVI, Encyclical Letter on Christian Love *Deus caritas est* (December 25, 2005), §35.

note in her calendar every Wednesday that simply reads: "Sunday." The note reminds her to initiate a brief discussion about the coming Sabbath day. What Mass will we be going to? Who might we have over? What might we do for family time? Proper preparation for Sunday provokes a change in the way we handle our Saturday. We make sure we get weekend chores done on Saturday so that Sunday can be free of them. We try to avoid the kinds of Saturday activities—binge entertainment, staying up late, drinking too much—that will make celebrating on Sunday more difficult. We also prepare the house for the next day's feast. On Saturday evening we dress the kitchen table with a runner, candles, a cross, a bible, and whatever else we might need for our celebration. If we are really planning well, we will get to Confession on Saturday afternoon, a practice that helps greatly in keeping the Lord's Day holy.

**2. Technology Fast:** On Sundays, our family becomes "techno-sabbatarian." We turn off our screens and give our devices a break. We have found that our smartphones connect us to everything but our souls, and often strangely remove us from the presence of the people next to us. This is not absolute but still a general rule. We may watch a film or a game together but still find that the less electronic devices present on Sunday the better.

**3. Sabbath Prayer:** We have added a ritual element to our Sunday by beginning the Lord's Day with the lighting of an oil lamp and reciting a Sabbath prayer. This ritual is a powerful entrance into receiving the Lord's Day and all its possibilities.

## SUNDAY MORNING PRAYER

*Blessed art Thou, O Lord our God, King of the Universe, Creator of all that is.*
*You have sanctified this day having made us for Yourself, and so we kindle the light to mark it as Holy,*
*a day set apart to honor and to celebrate Your work of creation and our redemption won through Your Son!*

*We pray this day may bring blessings of joy and peace to our hearts as we put workday thoughts and cares aside. Let the brightness of this Lord's Day light shine forth to tell that the divine spirit of love abides within our home. In its light may all our blessings be enriched, all our grief and trials softened. We pray in intercession for the needs and care of Your Church as we gather in freedom to worship—priests, ministers and religious, sons and daughters all over the world, together with the angels and saints—united as Your body. We pray for Christian unity and that all people will come to know Your unmeasurable love for them. We pray especially today for those who are suffering and in most need.*

*We pray in thanksgiving for this day inviting us to trust in Your providential care and join You in rest—a day to lay down our own work, worry, anxiety, need for productivity, and our own striving—in order that we might abide with*

*You, in freedom and peace. Bless all the activities of our day that it might be a time of refreshment, renewed joy and relationships, a day to delight in Your gift of love.*

*Father, with grateful hearts we set aside time today to give You praise, rejoice,*
*and enter Your rest, remembering who we are in Your creation, and observing with hope born of your death and resurrection. Amen.*

**4. Mass:** Given life's complications, the simple act of getting to Mass can sometimes be a great achievement! In heading to Mass, we try to be conscious of the specific act of getting there, which is a little pilgrimage. We like to think of the people all over the world (as well as the saints and angels!) mobilizing to gather as the Church, one family in Christ. We remember that job titles, social prestige, and positions related to wealth and privilege are put aside when we gather together as brothers and sisters equal before the Lord. Sharing the Eucharist together is at the heart of our Sunday. According to the Church, the Eucharist is "the source and summit of the Christian life,"[19] so we try to make it the source and summit of our lives as well with the high point on the Sabbath day.

**5. Sabbath Walk:** We try to find a time each Sunday to take a walk together as a couple and if possible as a

---

[19] Second Vatican Council, *Lumen gentium*, §11.

family. Depending on the circumstances of the day, we do this either in the morning before Mass or in the afternoon just after brunch. Whatever the time, it is always good to get outside. Walks are opportunities to talk together as well as to be silent. In the middle of our walk we usually pray the rosary. All sorts of surprising and sometimes difficult things arise during these walks, but we have never regretted taking them.

**6. Feast/Brunch:** Eating together is a very important part of our Sundays, although it is important that no one is overly burdened by meal preparation. We also take our time over our meals. We Americans can learn things from the Italians and other Europeans who take their meals in courses, one dish at a time. Meals are more leisurely and provide time for conversation and the renewing of relationship.

**7. Play/Games/Activities:** Sunday is also meant to be a time of joy and play. This can take a wide variety of expressions. We like board games, especially the kind that invite conversation. Our family's competitive spirit can sometimes get the best of us, and our games can turn into pitched battles. Other activities might include crafts, sports, picnics, canoeing, parks, the zoo, and music.

**8. Charity/Volunteer:** I remember that when I was a kid, our family would often visit the elderly on Sundays, especially those with no relatives. In particular, I remember going to Mrs. Delaney's house. The free time of Sunday provides an opportunity to visit people in a way that is not rushed or perfunctory.

The above list is a snapshot of our family Sunday keeping. There are many ways to incarnate Sabbath habits, and lots of room for creativity in finding the best way to live Sunday. Whatever pattern we may develop, the point is to help us to set aside the Sabbath day as a special gift to us, one with the capacity to foster our ability to truly rest, to celebrate the goodness of God and the world, and to revitalize our relationships with the most important people in our lives.

## CONCLUSION

In referring to the Lord's Day, John Paul II wrote, "Do not be afraid to give your time to Christ!"[20] While many of us do not put it in terms of fear, I think John Paul is right. We have to face our fears in relation to how we live the Lord's Day.

In a talk I gave years ago in Omaha to Catholic executives, the topic of the Lord's Day came up and a CEO in the group confessed he that could not conceivably stop working on Sundays. He went to Mass and had brunch with his family, but by early afternoon, was back at work. He responded that he was afraid of what would happen on Monday, afraid of not being competitive with his compet-

---

[20] John Paul II, "Homily for the Solemn Inauguration of the Pontificate" (October 22, 1978), 5: AAS 70 (1978), 947, quoted in *Dies Domini*.

itors who always work on Sunday.

His fears were real. As we move into a total work culture, many leaders and companies have found living the Lord's Day increasingly difficult. Certain companies, however, have been creative and courageous and bold in how seriously they take the Sabbath commandment. Chick-fil-A has achieved notoriety in its orientation to the Lord's Day. It is one of the few fast food chains that is closed on Sundays. This is the company's policy because its founder, Truett Cathy, a committed Christian, believes that all his employees need a weekly day of rest.

The striking fact about Chick-fil-A has been its success. Closing for one day out of seven means cutting out more than fourteen percent of their days of operation; and given that the day involved is Sunday, a popular day for eating out, the percentage of loss would seem even higher. Yet in 2016, Chick-fil-A's average sales per restaurant were four times higher than those of Kentucky Fried Chicken (KFC), which is open seven days a week.

What gives Chick-fil-A its advantage? It starts with a clear purpose and a leader's commitment to pursuing the company's purpose in thought and action. As Cathy once explained, "We aren't in the chicken business, we are in the people business."[21] And because they are in the people

---

[21] See Tiffany Greenway, "Truett Cathy's Unexpected Approach to Business and Life," *The Chicken Wire* (blog), November 9, 2015, https://thechickenwire.chick-fil-a.com/Inside-Chick-fil-A/Inspire-

business, they take seriously the deepest dimensions of our humanity, which includes rest. And so, as John Paul II writes, let us rediscover Sunday, which is a grace to not only "live the demands of faith to the full, but also so that we may respond concretely to the deepest human yearnings. Time given to Christ is never time lost, but is rather time gained, so that our relationships and indeed our whole life may become more profoundly human."[22]

More-People-Truett-Cathys-Unexpected-Approach-to-Business-and-Life.

[22] John Paul II, *Dies Domini*, §7.

·✦·

# Epilogue

One of the great blessings of my life has been the opportunity to build a new interdisciplinary program at the University of St. Thomas called Catholic Studies. The founder of the program, Don Briel, was an extraordinary intellectual with profound faith. In our work together for over twenty years, which had its fair share of frustrations and hardships, he would remind me that at the end of the day there are two kinds of people: those who are resentful and those who are grateful.

Those who are resentful see life not in terms of gift but of exchange—what they get out of life is what they put into it; which is why they find themselves resentful at the end of their lives. They are resentful that others have not earned their own. They are resentful they have been cheated from getting more. They reflect Adam I's alienation from Adam II. They are careerists without contemplation. And their achievements and money eventually betray them.

Those who are grateful, however, have a profound sense that they have been given much, and because of this gift, they accept they are also asked to give much. Those who are grateful often have the same set of problems, conflicts, and disappointments as everyone else. They find even within their suffering, however, a gift that does not embitter them but creates even greater compassion and love for others.

Our gratitude brings us to the deepest sense of ourselves through the relationship of what is received and given. To receive is a grace of God's love given to us in gifts, talents, desires, and skills that are to be given in return for the good of others. This grace shapes us and gives us the deep sense that our talents and the successes of our companies are not ours alone. We stand on the shoulders of those who came before us, those who gave us the opportunity to build up the good and construct institutions that contribute to the common good.

Discerning our call in this pattern of receiving and giving is never a straight line determined once and for all. Rather, our call is full of surprises, confusions, desolations, and consolations, which is why we need to pray constantly. Thus I end this book with a prayer adapted from one of the great theological minds and spiritual writers of all of Christianity, Blessed John Henry Newman. This prayer goes to the roots of faith, the reality that our lives are a gift from God not to be grasped at, but participated in.

*God, You have created me*

*to do You some definite service:*

*You have committed some work to me*

*which You have not committed to another.*

*I have my mission—*

*I may never know it in this life,*

*but I shall be told in the next.*

*Somehow I am necessary for Your purposes:*

*as necessary as an Archangel in his.*

*I have a part in the great work;*

*I am a link in a chain,*

*a bond of connection between persons.*

*You have not created me for nothing.*

*I shall do good, I shall do Your work;*

*I shall be an angel of peace,*

*A preacher of truth in my own place.*

*Deign to fulfill Your high purposes in me.*

*I am here to serve You, to be Yours*

*to be Your instrument.*

*Amen.*[1]

---

[1] This prayer is adapted from the meditation written by John Henry Cardinal Newman, which I slightly adapted from http://epistle.us/inspiration/johnhenrynewman.html.